People are talking about . . .
One Million Arrows

"*One Million Arrows* is a great wake-up call for parents of this generation. If we want our children to take part in the powerful purpose and unique mission God has designed for them, we've got to take responsibility for raising our kids as disciples of Christ."

—Josh D. McDowell
Author and Speaker

"God has called His people to leave a legacy of godliness for the next generation. *One Million Arrows* picks up on that high calling and casts a God-sized vision for parents who long to see their children used by God in mighty ways. I believe it will motivate you to invest in the lives of orphans and it will challenge you to raise your children as ambassadors for Christ rather than casualties of the culture-war."

—Dennis Rainey
President, FamilyLife

"The spiritual and physical needs of children in other countries—especially the orphaned and abandoned—are enormous. However, by investing in them, we can make a great difference in our world. As shown in *One Million Arrows*, many of these children are becoming evangelists and church planters for Christ's glory. I encourage you and your family to pray and become involved as God leads you."

—Franklin Graham
President and CEO, BGEA and Samaritan's Purse

"As parents, we need to encourage our teens to stand against the negative media that is constantly trying to influence them. *One Million Arrows* is a must read for parents who aspire to disciple their kids as world changers, recreating culture around them."

—Ron Luce
President and Founder, Teen Mania Ministries

"Every once in a while, an opportunity comes along that's so big and breath-taking—and so justifiably right—you have to say, 'Okay, you got me. Where do I sign up?' Such is the opportunity Julie Ferwerda unpacks in *One Million Arrows*."

—Dr. John Hull
President and CEO, EQUIP and ISS
(INJOY Stewardship Services)

"*One Million Arrows* is not just a book . . . it's part of a vision that's already taking place on every continent in the lives of God's young people. If you're ready for you and your family to truly make a difference in this world, this book is for you."

—Dr. Alvin Reid
Professor of Evangelism and
Associate Dean for Proclamation,
Southeastern Baptist Theological Seminary

"As seen in *One Million Arrows*, God is doing something special in this generation—He's stirring the hearts of our children, urging them to be ready and willing to become part of a mighty movement. Read this book, and embrace the power and phenomenal beauty of parenting your children for a special purpose. May we get our families involved to love those less fortunate than we are, and may the seriousness of discipling our children and grandchildren become a reality of doing and not just talking."

—Thelma Wells
Founder, A Woman of God Ministries and
National Conference Speaker

"I speak both as a father and a missionary to orphans; *One Million Arrows* deals with the most important issue facing the evangelical world today, and that is making disciples of our own children instead of expecting someone else to do it while we pursue other things. There is no more urgent pursuit, no more essential need than raising our children to know and love Christ."

—Clayton King
Founder and President, Crossroads Worldwide

"*One Million Arrows* provides a challenge we all need to hear. If you care about children and if you want them to change their world, this book is a must. Telling real stories about real people, Julie Ferwerda provides practical and exciting ideas about how to position our children above the selfish mediocrity that brands so many kids. This book shows what's possible with a God who can make all things possible. I love it and want to live it and share it with my friends. Thank you, Julie, for giving parents a challenge and a strategy for raising kids who can change their world for God."

—Dr. Steve Stephens
Marriage and Family Psychologist, Author

"It has been my honor to work with Julie Ferwerda, a follower of Christ whose passion for her faith shines brightly in her writing. I am always on the lookout for books that encourage American believers to remember the world outside their own communities. Julie's *One Million Arrows* reminds us that being a neighbor to the physically and spiritually downtrodden is a vital part of our personal walk with the Lord. Her book was a blessing to me personally as I consider both the practical application of this aspect of my faith, and how I will instill in my children a fervor to show God's love to the people outside their own culture."

—Stephen McGarvey
Executive Editor, Crosswalk.com and Christianity.com

"Julie Ferwerda's vision for *One Million Arrows* needs to be heard and caught by the Christian community of the 21st century. She rightly senses that we live in a time of great opportunity for the advance of God's Kingdom, but it will take daring, commitment, and sacrifice to make it happen—along with the wisdom to start young and focus on the children of this generation. Anyone passionately committed to advancing God's kingdom should read this."

—David Guzik
Director of Calvary Chapel Bible College, Germany
Author of David Guzik's Bible Commentary

ONE MILLION
ARROWS

"One Million Arrows ... casts a God-sized vision for parents who long to see their children used by God in mighty ways." —Dennis Rainey

RAISING YOUR CHILDREN TO CHANGE THE WORLD

JULIE FERWERDA

WinePress Publishing (PO Box 428, Enumclaw, WA 98022) functions only as book publisher. As such, the ultimate design, content, editorial accuracy, and views expressed or implied in this work are those of the author.

Author's note: This book contains extensive author interviews during 2007–2008, both nationally and internationally. All quotes, unless otherwise referenced, are taken directly from those interviews.

All Scripture quotations, unless otherwise indicated, are taken from the *Holy Bible, New Living Translation*®, NLT®. Copyright © 1996, 2004. Used by permission of Tyndale House Publishers, Inc., Carol Stream, Illinois 60188. All rights reserved.

Scripture quotations marked NIV are taken from the *Holy Bible, New International Version*®, NIV®. Copyright © 1984 by International Bible Society. Used by permission of Zondervan. All rights reserved.

Scripture quotations marked AMP are taken from the *Amplified Bible*®, copyright © 1987 by The Lockman Foundation. Used by permission.

Scripture quotations marked MSG are taken from *The Message*, copyright © 2004 by NavPress Publishing Group. Used by permission.

Printed in the United States of America.

ISBN 13: 978-1-60615-011-5
ISBN 10: 1-60615-011-1
Library of Congress Catalog Card Number: 2009924987

Children born to a young man are like sharp arrows in a warrior's hands.
How happy is the man whose quiver is full of them!
—Psalm 127:4-5

For Papa. You are the closest thing to God's love I've ever known in this world. May your vision of one million arrows for God be something you see with your very own eyes on this side of eternity. Thank you for choosing to do the hard things so that you might be used to bring hope, inspiration, and purpose into the lives of parents and children on every continent.

This book is also dedicated to all of the wonderful orphan ministries worldwide that are gathering once purposeless children and sharpening them as arrows for the Kingdom to finish the most important work in this world—fulfilling The Great Commission.

And for my own nearly honed arrows, Danielle and Jessica—I am so proud of you, and I know that you both are going to continue to light up the world for Jesus.

In honor of Dr. M.A. Thomas' (Papa's) vision, all proceeds from this book are designated for international orphan arrow ministry.

CONTENTS

INTRODUCTION

Have you ever wondered if there's a grander purpose for our children, beyond growing up to become responsible, productive adults who happen to be Christians? There is! It's absolutely true! Our kids can be trained to become part of an epic, spiritual movement in our day. Through role modeling, training, and encouragement, they can become part of a vision to deliver a more profound and eternal impact on this world than we ever thought possible.

Our guiding light shines from many individuals, families, and ministries who have blazed the trail before us. One man in particular, a father of many world-changers, will personally guide us through this book with his revolutionary vision: *one million arrows for God*—one million children gathered, sharpened, and launched to make an eternal difference in their communities, cultures, countries, and even the world at large.

Please note that this book is not promoting any particular ministry, but it's a vision and a *mission* all families can take part in together. What is this *mission*? It has echoed through the centuries, from the words of Moses all the way to the words of God's own Son 1,500 years later. In my own words, this God-given mission imparted by Jesus goes something like this: "Even after I'm gone from this place, I want you to go and teach people how to be My followers. First, start with your children. Train them to follow Me, and then train them by example to help others follow Me—family, friends, classmates, and neighbors. Then think about how your family might bring My love and the Good News of My salvation to your community and even your country. But don't stop there! I will show you how your family can impact others around the world, until all nations have heard about Me and have been told of My gift of eternal life! Yes, I will use your children to change the world with My love ... *if you show them the way.*"

PART I
GATHER

We will not hide these truths from our children

but will tell the next generation about the
glorious deeds of the LORD.

We will tell of His power and the mighty miracles He did.

For He issued His decree to Jacob; He gave His law to Israel.

He commanded our ancestors to teach them to their children,

so the next generation might know them—

even the children not yet born—

that they in turn might teach their children.

So each generation can set its hope anew on God,

remembering His glorious miracles and obeying His commands.

Then they will not be like their ancestors—

stubborn, rebellious, and unfaithful,

refusing to give their hearts to God.

—Psalm 78:4–8

CHAPTER 1

DETERMINE YOUR COURSE

And you must love the LORD your God with all your heart, all your soul, and all your strength. And you must commit yourselves wholeheartedly to these commands I am giving you today. Repeat them again and again to your children ... Write them on the doorposts of your house and on your gates.
—Deuteronomy 6:5–9

Destiny is not a matter of chance. It is a matter of choice.
—William Jennings Bryan[1]

What were you doing on 9/11?

I'd just cranked up the tunes and hopped on my Nordic Track as part of my normal morning routine, when my husband called from work to tell me to turn on the TV. Watching the events unfold, I don't think I've ever felt as helpless or as horrified as I did that day. The world no longer seemed like the safe, secure place I thought it was only one day before. In the worst way, I wanted to keep my two girls, ages seven and ten, out of school that day to protect them and reassure them until the danger had passed.

For the rest of that day, and many more to come, the surreal sights on TV haunted me: planes striking the buildings; massive explosions; the sudden, momentary collapse—twice—of 110 floors of elaborately constructed concrete, steel, and glass that took years to erect; and the mountains of debris that smoked and smoldered for many days. But nothing shook me as much as the unforgettable images of human bodies spilling out of the buildings like grains of rice. Neither those who lived through it, nor those of us who watched the shocking events unfold on TV, will ever forget.

One young man I read about, Cary Sheih, a technical consultant from New York, barely made it out alive. Working on a project for the Port Authority of New York and New Jersey at his 72nd floor desk, he'd just finished his usual mid-morning PB&J, when he heard an explosion, followed by tremendous building sways and vibrations. At first, he thought it might be an earthquake, so he dashed to the stairwell, where a quick, but calm, evacuation was underway. As people made their way down, some received messages on their cell phones that an airplane had accidentally crashed into the building, but there was no mention of a terrorist attack.

With the heavy, choking stench of jet fuel, descending the tower proved difficult. But if it was difficult for him, he couldn't imagine how difficult it was for the rescue crews he passed, huffing their way up an endless corkscrew of stairs and then hurrying back down, carrying badly injured and burned victims. He recalls, "Sometime around the 30th or 40th floor, we passed the first firefighters coming up the stairs. They reassured people that we were safe and that we would all get out fine. By this point, they were absolutely breathless, but still pushing upward, slowly and unyieldingly, one step at a time. I could only imagine how tired they were, carrying their axes, hoses, and heavy outfits, climbing up all those stairs. Young men started offering [to help] the firemen to carry up their gear for a few flights, but they all refused. Each and every one of them."[2]

As Cary neared the bottom, the building began to shake and sway again, the lights flickered out, and eerie sounds of buckling steel accompanied screams of people falling down the stairwell. After being assisted by firemen through darkness to a different stairwell, a panicked Cary somehow made it down the last few flights to safety, where his wildest imagination couldn't have prepared him for what he encountered. The burning trees, wreckage, fireballs, and dust resembled *a war zone.*

While reading through this and other accounts concerning 9/11, I noticed an inspiring, recurrent theme. While there were many, many heroes and selfless individuals working tirelessly to assist throughout this tragic period, it was the *firemen* who undoubtedly made some of the greatest sacrifices of all, and whose ultimate acts of bravery impacted lives worldwide. While most everyone else scrambled for the exit signs to save themselves (which I'm positive I would have done, too), these rescue workers fearlessly *headed up into the towering infernos* that day, many likely aware that they might not make it out alive.

Most kids see firefighters as larger than life heroes, which is probably why many of them want to be one when they grow up. Who wouldn't want to be thought of as a hero, especially one that saved lives? I came across a touching book report that was written about 9/11 by three kids:

> The firefighters of 9/11 are heroes because they have saved the lives of hundreds of people, while they knew the building could collapse. While you go up a burning, 110-story building you would be very scared, because you'll think of your own life. When you are a firefighter you mustn't think too much about your own life or you may not be able to save lives. Being a hero means saving lives. That's the difference between being a celebrity and being a hero. Why would a celebrity be important to you? It is just someone with a well-paying job. You'll be someone's hero if you help him with his or her life.[3]

As I think about what these insightful kids have so magnificently articulated about the qualities of firemen, particularly the 9/11 firemen, I'm deeply moved with admiration and respect. In an emergency, firemen are:

- First responders, well-trained, and ready to save lives, even at the expense of their own.
- Purposeful and deliberate, aware that lives are at stake and time is short.
- Doggedly determined, knowing that the more lives they can save the better.
- Regarded in both life and death as the heroes of this world.

No one involved in 9/11 could disagree with this assessment. Remembering the expressions of both courage and fear etched on rescue workers' faces as they spoke reassuringly to guide many people to safety, Cary Sheih said, "I am so grateful for the courage of the firemen and policemen who gave up their lives to help us down the burning tower. As I relive this moment over and over in my mind, I can't help but think that these courageous firemen already knew in their minds that they would not make it out of the building alive, and that they didn't want to endanger any more civilians or prevent one less person from making it to safety."[4]

While they will undoubtedly go down in history as larger than life heroes, we can't forget how human and vulnerable they were, too. I have looked through their pictures online. Most of them were young family men, with their whole lives ahead of them—men who kissed their own babies goodnight on Monday for the last time so that those they helped to safety could kiss their kids goodnight many more nights to come. They unknowingly said final goodbyes to their own families Tuesday morning so that many others could come home to their families that night.

In the moment of the realization of the grave danger, it had to be a dilemma for the firemen, choosing between lion-hearted courage and paralyzing, self-protective fear. How were they able to do it? Was it because it was their job? Because their buddies were doing it? Because their captain told them to do it? What exactly is it that leads a person to choose a profession where courage must prevail when all pretenses and rewards are stripped away in the face of death?

More than a job identity or a paycheck, more than an obligation or a hope of any kind of recognition, firemen are willing to risk their lives and to face their fears because they are motivated by something far greater than fear.

The Bible refers to this motivating force as *love*! Authentic, selfless love drives away fear (1 John 4:18). And it was the love—not the duty—of those firemen and emergency workers that truly made them heroes of the day, both the ones who died and the ones who worked doggedly through the wreckage, many suffering permanent damage to their lungs and bodies. And that kind of sacrifice, according to Jesus Christ, is love at its very best. "I command you to love each other in the same way that I love you. And here is how to measure it—*the greatest love is shown when people lay down their lives for their friends*" (John 15:12–13, emphasis mine).

Firemen of Life

So what does all this talk about 9/11 and firemen have to do with parenting? If you're a follower of Christ and you want to raise children who are also followers of Christ, quite a lot. And if you want to entertain the possibility of raising children who will change the world around them, and even the world at large, everything!

It's no secret that every day on this earth, countless lives are at stake. People are dying every day who do not know Jesus, and almost just as bad, people are *living* every day who do not know Jesus. I don't know about you, but I cannot imagine struggling through the hardships, losses, disappointments, and sorrows of this world without the comfort and peace of knowing Jesus and His love. And we know that someday soon, this world full of magnificent structures, along with all the people who have not put their faith in Christ, will collapse in a catastrophic fire (Zephaniah 1:18).

In other words, time is running out.

The seriousness of that reality raises some questions: What is my family here for? As believers, is parenting a more significant and eternity-impacting role than we've given it credit for? Are we satisfied with happy, well-adjusted, even ambitious kids who happen to love God, or is there something more?

It is at this crossroads that we will explore the invitation we've been offered—a divine invitation to become a part of His-Story. As this story unfolds throughout the space of our lives, which role will our family accept in this cosmic emergency? Hopefully not the victims. Hopefully not the ones running scared to save ourselves (and I am absolutely not criticizing those who made it out on 9/11—this is for spiritual application only). Hopefully not uninvolved bystanders who are disinterested, unable, or ill-equipped to do anything but watch.

I've realized that, in the grand scheme of life, more than just raising my kids to "keep the faith," I want to raise my kids to save lives. *I want to raise firemen.* Not necessarily the earthly fire-fighting kind, but the heavenly fire-fighting kind. Kids who are well-trained and ready to help save as many lives as possible. Kids who grow up, remembering at the forefront of everything they do, that time is short and lives are at stake, and who will one day be seen as spiritual heroes for helping many lives to safety.

I want to raise kids who love like Jesus.

Just think what it would be like to have kids who grow up in this self-destructing world with brave faces and hope in their voices, carrying within their hearts the ambition of bringing as many people as possible safely into the Kingdom. I believe that this kind of holy ambition is the secret to life at its best, and I want my kids to experience this kind of life. Jesus said, "If you try to keep your life for yourself, you will lose it. But if you give up your life for me, you will find true life" (Matthew 16:25). And therein, we hear the invitation: *Will you raise your kids to be firemen? Will you be a fireman for God's sake?* We may never be called to die for Jesus like so many others in our world today, but we are still called to a holy rescue mission—to live sacrificially for God so that others will be led to safety through our loving assistance.

Rebels with a Cause

I recently met two brothers, both firemen of the Kingdom variety, who understand about saving lives by choosing to deliberately head into burning buildings. For them, the rescue mission all started with a small idea and a heart to snatch their fellow teens from a dangerous culture.

At age sixteen, twins Alex and Brett Harris decided to start a little blog in their spare time over the summer called *TheRebelution.com*, with the intent of *starting a teenage rebellion*. "The word 'rebelution' is a combination of the words 'rebellion' and 'revolution,'" explains Brett. "So it carries a sense of an uprising against social norms. But in this case, it's not a rebellion against God-established authority, but against the low expectations of our society. It's a refusal to be defined by our ungodly, rebellious culture." To their astonishment, within a couple years, their site had received over 14 million hits, becoming the most popular Christian teen blog on the web.

As a follow up, they decided to write a book for teens called *Do Hard Things*, exhorting young people not to take the easy way out, but to do those things that seem harder now but have a bigger payoff in the end (as in "delayed gratification"). Since then, God has opened doors for them to speak to thousands of teens nationwide through conferences that are planned, organized, and run primarily by youth.

More than just a website, *The Rebelution* is both a mindset and a movement. "Our goal," according to the brothers, "is to create a community of young people where thinking deeply is the norm, and where achieving excellence is 'cool.' History says young people can be doing big things *right now*! Don't let the culture's expectations toward teenagers dictate what you think is possible. The teen years are not a vacation from responsibility. They are the training ground of future leaders who dare to be responsible now."[5]

Whether from media, parents, authority figures, or peers, low expectations have become the rule for this generation, rather than the exception. Not only are kids expected *not* to possess admirable character or useful competence, but also they are expected to do the opposite. *The Rebelution* defies this kind of thinking by calling out youth to return to biblical and historical levels of character and competence as exhorted by Paul in 1 Timothy 4:12: "Don't let anyone think less of you because you are young. Be an example to all believers in what you teach, in the way you live, in your love, your faith, and your purity."

Their message, based on their belief that God is raising up their generation for global change, is a passionate call back to excellence, purpose, and significance for young people. It's not about doing *more* things, or inflicting oneself with toilsome chores; it's about lifestyle choices that will often take you out of your comfort zone and into places where you are focused on using your abilities and resources to encourage and benefit others . . . ultimately to save lives.

"Brett and I firmly believe we are living in historic times," Alex says. "We further believe that God is raising up a generation of young people who will one day assume positions of leadership in all spheres of life: social, political, and spiritual. This is not a call for the complacent or the lackadaisical. This is not a call to those who are willing to lower their standards to meet the expectations of their culture. *This is a call to the rebelutionary.*"

Initially I wondered how two kids could possibly have achieved so many bold and bright accomplishments, not to mention how they've acquired more wisdom than many adults. Was it handed to them? Do they harbor a special gene pool (their parents might agree with that notion)? Did they turn out like this by chance?

Actually, Alex and Brett would probably be ordinary kids, except for one thing. They had parents who believed in making the sacrifices necessary to raise their kids to make a difference. Kids who, in turn, learned to make sacrifices in order to serve others. They had parents who devoted themselves to raising *firemen*. Keeping this at the forefront of their parenting strategy, Mom and Dad Harris raised kids who understood and accepted the fact that it was going to take a lot of hard work for everyone in order to succeed in this goal. As a result of this mentality, these young men have literally started a *Rebelution* across our nation . . . and our world.

There are actually two other grown children from the Harris home. One of them, Joshua, became a best-selling author at the age of twenty, with the book *I Kissed Dating Goodbye* (Multnomah 1997). He went on to write more bestsellers, developed purity seminars for young people, and toured as a national conference speaker in front of hundreds of thousands of young people, calling them out of their culture to a lifestyle of purity. At age twenty-seven, he became the senior pastor of a large church, where he still serves today.

In 2002, another brother, Joel, launched the Northwest Academy of Worship Music to help raise up worship leaders and worship teams for local churches in the Portland area, where over 150 students of all ages have been successfully trained. Since 2007, he's also been using his music skills to lead worship for *The Rebelution Tour*.

As I got to know the Harris family, I saw that "chance" and "opportunity" had nothing to do with their parenting success. "If our teen years have been different than most," says Alex, "it's not because we are somehow better than other teens, but because we've been motivated by that simple but very big idea filtering down from our parents' example and training: *Do hard things*."

With four out of four grown children serving the Lord and significantly impacting their world, it's obvious that the Harrises are doing something right. And I've discovered that this "something" is available to all parents. Throughout this book, we're going to visit with more parents like these to find out exactly what they are doing to shape godly kids who are ready and able to help save lives, no matter what their limitations or circumstances. Turning out kids like these is not just possible—it's possible for you and your family with just a few moderate but important lifestyle changes.

Parenting is, really, at the heart of Jesus' command for discipleship. It's teaching our kids to live with Jesus and to love like Jesus. It does require a cost, as anything worthwhile does, but that cost will be far outweighed by the benefits and rewards. God has created our kids with unique abilities, gifts, and desires for a very special purpose. All they need now is to be trained and ready, available for divinely appointed opportunities.

So now it's time to ask: Do we truly want to give our kids the best of everything we have to offer in the short time we have to impact their lives? Do we want our kids to live—and someday die—the spiritual heroes of this world? If we have answered "yes," then it's time to learn about a vision for our families that's so amazing; it will change the course of history.

My discovery all started on a little trip I took to northwest India.

CHAPTER 2

JOIN THE VISION

Then the Lord told Abram, "Leave your country, your relatives, and your father's house, and go to the land that I will show you. I will cause you to become the father of a great nation. I will bless you and make you famous, and I will make you a blessing to others. . . . All the families of the earth will be blessed through you."

—Genesis 12:1–3

God said that all children are arrows in the hands of the mighty Man, Jesus Christ. All we have to do in order to evangelize the whole world is to take the arrows and place them into Jesus' hands.

—Dr. M.A. Thomas (Papa)[1]

In February 2007, I was about to discover the special vision from a revolutionary parent that would totally change my life. It all started when I had an unexpected invitation to go to India to teach at a writers' conference. But when that fell through after I'd already purchased my plane ticket, some fluky circumstances brought about a chance for me to go to northwest India for some freelance writing opportunities. It was there that I met and spent significant time with a man named Mullanakuzhiyil Abraham Thomas (not conducive to rhymed poetry). Only a few days into my trip, I was absolutely certain this was a divine appointment.

Now in his early seventies, M.A. Thomas, known as "Papa" to many thousands throughout India and even the world, came across as a simple, warm, unhurried man, who was genuinely interested in others. In fact, even after talking to him for several days, I had no idea that he'd earned many accolades as an influential leader throughout India for his extensive and widespread ministries to the downtrodden. The Padma Shri Award (one of the highest Indian civilian awards) for humanitarian contribution, the Mahatma Gandhi Award for his work with the needy, and his Mother Teresa Award for social justice are all proof of his deep love and committed service to his countrymen. Most political and ministry leaders within India are quite familiar with M.A. Thomas, yet I found him to be completely unimpressed with himself, and most everything I learned about his achievements came from others.

As my month-long trip to India progressed, I learned about Papa's extreme visionary parenting. In the role of a loving father, he's bringing about change in India and throughout the world. While his early work as a missionary and church planter began in 1960, he later began rescuing orphaned and abandoned children off the streets of India in 1978, and raising them in his "Hope Homes." In these homes, they experience family love and belonging, and receive a top-rate education, as well as the opportunity and training to become disciples and servants of Christ. Since then, Papa's "father of the fatherless" ministry has become one of the largest Christian ministries in India, with over 21,000 pastors and missionaries trained and sent to the mission field, a majority of them once abandoned children. His ministry has also expanded to the countries of Malawi and Haiti.

The call on Papa's life for missions came when he was twenty years old and in Bible college in Madras, India (now called Chennai). While attending a special conference, he heard a message taken from Isaiah 6:8: "Whom will I send? Who will go for us?" That night, the unmistakable voice of the Holy Spirit extended the invitation to him, and he willingly gave his dreams and future to God in total surrender. Not long after that, God directed him through fasting and prayer to go to Rajasthan, a state in northwest India with very little, if any, Christian influence back in the 1960s.

The day before his Bible college graduation, Papa didn't have the money to travel to Rajasthan, but he was still determined to obey God and leave for his mission the very next day. Later that same day, a man came to the campus to recruit Papa to head up the India branch of his American ministry. The job offered great perks: a comfortable salary, rent money, and even medical expenses. This established ministry is well-known today as Campus Crusade. The man offering Papa the job? *Bill Bright*.

"Dr. Bright," Papa responded, "if you'd asked me six months ago, I would have joined you. But I have promised my Lord that I will go to north India to pioneer a mission, and to establish churches. Even though God hasn't given me train fare yet, I'm not going to change my promise to Him." If the money didn't come in, Papa and his newly pregnant wife had already made the decision together to walk more than 1,400 miles to his destination, despite her morning sickness. Is it any surprise that the money for train fare miraculously came in from many sources, just in time for departure?

Inspired by the faith and obedience of his fellow evangelist, Bill Bright graciously offered to pay $25 a month for Papa's rent for the first year on the mission field, where Papa began devoting his life to this spiritually dark and hostile region. Only two weeks after he arrived, he began enduring persecution by radical anti-Christians, a reality that has continued throughout his ministry to this day. Beatings, burned Bibles and churches, constant threats, rapes, expensive legal cases, financial penalties, imprisonment, and sometimes martyrdom have been forms of mistreatment for practically all mission-minded Christians in this and many other parts of India.

In the early years after moving to Rajasthan, he began establishing churches and Bible institutes to train willing new believers to be missionaries and church planters. His biggest desire was to train enough missionaries and pastors to go to every village and city in India that had never heard about Jesus—a number estimated at as many as 600,000 back in those days.

As these native workers went out to set up community worship centers—multi-purpose centers for church and outreach projects—each center would, in time, build Christian schools and medical facilities. This led to more worship centers being built in neighboring communities, and provided more students interested in attending Bible college to go to even more villages and cities.

It was a brilliant plan, but there was one huge obstacle. It was a painstakingly slow process finding enough young men and women who were ready and willing to devote their lives to full-time Christian service in this capacity. Of the new believers trickling into the fold from Papa's evangelizing efforts, many had spouses, families, or other earthly ties that held them back from becoming a part of his colossal dream, not to mention many were deterred by the threat of persecution. It all seemed impossible.

A Multitude for Jesus

More than fifteen years later, in the late 1970s, Papa began asking God what could be done about all the orphaned, abandoned, and desperate children he saw every day scrounging on the streets or even "selling" themselves just to acquire the basic necessities of life. Their sadness became his sadness as he imagined a life with no love or educational opportunities to escape the hopeless prison they were born into.

Especially tugging at his heart were the kids growing up in leprosy-affected colonies, because, even more than most, they had zero chance for a successful future. It's hard to estimate how many leprosy-affected live in India—the highest of any country—but it's in the millions. Because of pervasive religious superstitions in their culture, leprosy-affected people are thought of as being punished for being evil in a previous life. No one wants to touch them or show them kindness, because it's believed they "deserve this lot in life." Any person showing them kindness or helping them in any way "comes under a curse." Leprosy-affected people and their children are considered the lowest of the low, and they are completely rejected by practically all of society.

Papa thought about the senselessness of their suffering. It was an ocean of a problem, one that could not be impacted at the adult level, since the effects of leprosy are visible and irreversible. However, leprosy usually takes years to be transmitted from parent to child. Papa realized that in order to make a difference, the answer would be to help their children break out of this cycle by removing them from the colony before it was too late. The children could be loved, nurtured, educated, and most importantly, given eternal hope through a personal relationship with Jesus Christ.

When they grew up and became confident, healthy citizens and educated leaders, they could spread the love of God wherever they lived and worked by demonstrating the power of the Gospel message with their redeemed lives. When they visited their homes, their parents would see their meaningful and successful lives and be drawn to the amazing, life-changing power of the Gospel. In this way, a true difference could be made for this large group of people.

And so, spurred on by the faith-based work of George Muller, a nineteenth century visionary who provided for 2,100 orphans daily by relying solely on God's provision through prayer, Papa decided to open up his own home as an orphanage—the first of many "Hope Homes"—for these kinds of children.

"Lord," he prayed, "if I had as many orphans and destitute children as Mr. Mueller, what a multitude they would be for Jesus Christ!" Papa would be able to spiritually train all the children who came to him, and to potentially acquire even more students someday for the Bible institutes—students who could have the opportunity to prepare to go to the villages who had never heard about Jesus as pastors, doctors, nurses, and teachers—all messengers of the Good News. It surely seemed to be the answer to Papa's nagging life question: *How do I find enough messengers to bring the love of Jesus to every people, tribe, nation, and language, according to Revelation 7:9?*

A God-Sized Vision

Usually when God is in the process of unfolding a plan in our lives, it gradually illuminates, like a dark landscape at sunrise. That's why it's crucial that we maintain our dependence on His daily guidance. Anyone can receive a promise or a vision and get busy working towards it on his or her own, but without the *continuous* guidance of the Holy Spirit, grand plans taken into our own hands fall flat, or worse, lead us into trouble. It's the faithful years of relationship with God, one prayer at a time, where great, world-changing work is accomplished.

In 1997, after nineteen years of faithful, daily dependence on God in orphan ministry, sometimes including as many as six hours of focused prayer in a given day, Papa reflected on God's leading in his life. By then he'd raised his sought after multitude of 2,000 children in the many Hope Homes now located across India, and he had personally trained many of them in his Bible institutes for full-time ministry. It was then that the Holy Spirit directed him to the verse that put the TNT to his dream, becoming his guiding light in ministry for the rest of his days on earth.

The verse was Psalm 127:3–5: "Behold, children are a heritage from the Lord, the fruit of the womb a reward. As arrows are in the hand of a warrior, so are the children of one's youth. Happy, blessed, and fortunate is the man whose quiver is filled with them!" (AMP).

Papa absolutely knew God was telling him something profound through this verse, because instead of bringing him comfort, it struck him with deep sadness. Yes, he had ministered to many children, but there were many millions more—maybe as many as 80 million in India alone—desperately scrounging and clawing their way through gutters, trying to find a life worth living on the streets, in train stations, in brothels, and in leper colonies, all of them unsuccessfully. *Lord, if children are your gift and reward to mankind, why are so many of them as broken and unwanted as dead branches? How could so many throw-aways of society become a blessing to anyone? What do you want me to do?*

And then the rest of the vision flooded in as bright light, deliberately and forcefully squeezing its way through an opening doorway. There was indeed a way that Papa could see his own lifelong dream fulfilled of establishing a Christian ministry in all of the cities and villages throughout India that had never heard about Jesus, while at the same time helping so many children become God's great gift and reward to this earth.

One million arrows for God.

As the picture waxed crystal clear, the sadness Papa felt was replaced by great joy! *Gather* one million broken branches—the native-born, orphaned, and abandoned children—*sharpen* them with education, faith, and a heart for The Great Commission (Matthew 28:18–20), and *launch* them like arrows back into all the regions of India that have never heard about Jesus. In fact, why limit it to India? Papa realized this model could work anywhere. There were many such broken branches worldwide that could do the same in their own native countries!

In the modern world, where western missionaries are being denied access into many countries and regions, who better appointed to bring the Gospel to transform villages, cities, and even countries with the love of Christ than the locals—those who already speak the language and know the culture as their own? The more he thought about it, the more Papa imagined that the redeeming work of God in these precious children's lives could be the beginning of a mighty movement, one that would someday bring a great multitude of souls into the Kingdom of God worldwide. And this great vision was well on its way since the Hope Homes had already been established for nearly twenty years.

Besides the benefits for each child—a redeemed past, a purposeful present, and a future living with Jesus in His Kingdom—these children were also a great benefit to the ministry because of their extreme devotion, lack of earthly ties, and gratitude toward Christ.

There are so many miraculous testimonies that display Papa's successful model in action, but one of my favorite pictures of the complete redemption potential, nineteen-year-old Napoleon, is sort of a modern-day Joseph story.

Napoleon lived a comfortable lifestyle with his family of five in a large South India city. But one day, when he was six years old, the police came and arrested his entire family, falsely accusing them of being Naxalites, or anti-government terrorists. Even though they were soon released without charges, the social pressures and superstitions present in India made them a threat to their friends and family. Overnight, they lost everything and everyone that mattered.

Packing few belongings, the family boarded a train. Later, when they stopped at a station, Napoleon watched his dad give his older brother and sister some money and send them off, he assumed for food. But the train left without them, and Napoleon never saw them again. Then, after the train got up to full speed, he watched in disbelief as his parents intentionally jumped off the train to their deaths. The train conductor told six-year-old Napoleon that, by law, he had to debark at the next station to claim the bodies and arrange having them removed from the station.

He spent the next year living on trains, cleaning floors and shining shoes to try to make enough money to eat. Once he rode the train farther than usual and ended up in a state where he couldn't speak the language, as each state in India has its own language. A seemingly caring woman spotted him and led him to a home, where she served him a plate of food.

Ravenous, he ate every bite. Only after the meal did he realize it was a set up—the woman turned him in to the police for stealing.

Napoleon spent the next ten years in a youth corrections facility, along with other kids who were mostly hardened criminals. During this time, a man came to visit him regularly and eventually led him to Christ, and then helped him get into one of Papa's orphanages where his faith blossomed.

"I'm so thankful to God for rescuing me," Napoleon, now a first-year student in Papa's main Bible college, says. "If He hadn't brought me here, I'd be an atheist by now, but God chose me and brought me here at the right moment so that I could know Him. My biggest desire is to become a state government official so that I can help the poor, underprivileged, and minority people."

Even with all the bad stuff that's happened to him, Napoleon's not bitter. "If God hadn't allowed me to get put into the juvenile corrections facility, I'd still be on the train, begging and shining shoes to survive. God used that experience to bring me to this place today so that I could help others."

It's no wonder that kids like Napoleon are willing to devote their lives to carry on Papa's legacy. Their gratitude for being rescued from the pit of death and despair is immense.

Passion and Vision Growing

Papa, an earthly father of the fatherless, has more children today than ever restored to the quiver of God's blessing to this earth because of his faithfulness. More than 16,000 broken children's lives have been gathered and restored through his love, with at least two-thirds of those devoting their lives to full-time ministry as pastors, evangelists, teachers, and medical professionals. Most of the others have become educated professionals and leaders, with a variety of respectable jobs, who also use their life vocations as a means to spread the Good News about Jesus Christ in their work places and communities. It is conservatively estimated that 95 percent of the grown Hope Home children are serving the Lord to this day, whether part time or full time.

And that's not all. In addition to all the children who have been rescued since the late 1970s, there are offshoots of this ministry reaching into many lives throughout India, including thousands of community worship centers in cities and villages; for-profit Christian schools (they help fund the orphanages); over one hundred small Bible institutes and two larger Bible colleges, from which over 21,000 students have graduated for the ministry; a major hospital; medical clinics; leprosy and prostitute outreaches; tsunami ministries; and more than seventy Hope Homes.

With all that work behind him, you'd think an aged man who has shepherded thousands of orphans and pastors would be ready to retire on a sunny beach with a stack of good reading material. How many of us would be thinking: *Isn't it time for someone else to take over and give me a break? I've done my time, and now, after almost fifty years of trials, persecutions, and intense labor, my momentum is waning. I'm ready to move on with my retirement!*

Like any devoted parent who never stops investing in his kids and grandkids, nothing could be further from reality for Papa. Retirement isn't in his vocabulary because he knows that earth is *the work*, and heaven is *the rest*. Even though his biological son, Samuel, is shouldering much of the workload and responsibility these days, Papa feels his dream growing more vivid and reachable by the day, and that's what keeps him pursuing the vision with excitement and energy. His critical job of fathering and discipling a multitude for Christ is far from finished, and he still wants to see the dream of *one million arrows for God* reached before he takes his last breath.

Today Papa says, "The Lord is preparing me and using me more now than ever before. I feel the closest presence and fellowship with Him, and I have more vision and more burden and more commitment than ever before."

Bringing Papa's Vision Home

Papa's vision is inspiring and revolutionary. His commitment to unwanted children is more than admirable. But that's in India. What does his story have to do with you and me? What does it have to do with us raising our children to be the world's heroes? Actually, his vision for raising arrows is a vision for all parents, and it's something that can and should happen in every country and every culture.

An arrow of God doesn't have to be in full-time ministry, but is always focused unwaveringly on bringing the love of Jesus Christ into every aspect of the journey throughout his or her life. Along with raising a daughter who might decide to become a heart surgeon, I also want to prepare her to be ready and able to be used as a healer of hearts. In addition to raising a child who decides to become a teacher, I also want to prepare her to be a disciple-maker of Christ. Instead of raising my girls to have an affinity for international travel, I'd like to take it a step further and give them the opportunity to develop a heart for missions. Instead of raising channel changers, I most definitely want to raise world changers.

"There is a difference between the man who goes into medicine because science, service, and humanity course through his veins, and the man who sees it as a lucrative career," Voddie Baucham, author of *Family Driven Faith*, explains. "One man is pursuing the best the world has to offer; the other is pursuing the best he has to offer the world."[2]

My biggest dream for my kids has become for them to always have at the core of everything they do—every motivation and thought—the desire to search for God's dreams for their lives, asking questions like: *How can I make a difference in this world? What did God create me to do on this planet to help accomplish His purposes? How can my life be truly fulfilling? How can I become an arrow for God?*

The Enemy wishes nothing more than to coax our kids, if not into rebellion, into pursuing passionless, insignificant, and potentially empty lives. As long as he can hamstring them with apathy, he need not worry about them doing damage to his kingdom. But now, like Papa, we've been given the exciting opportunity to raise arrows—weapons of warfare. Our kids have been put on this earth for a great purpose and a *mission*.

But we can hardly sit back and think that our kids are the only ones singled out for such grand plans. How will they know unless we teach them from our own habits and experiences? How will they catch it unless we model it for them consistently? Just like Papa, God wants to use the shepherds and shapers of *His children* to bring about change by raising them to become—as we are becoming—sharp arrows in the hands of Jesus Christ, prepared as skillful weapons against the kingdom of darkness.

Remember, there's a war going on in the heavenlies. Our children can either be pawns unaware, or they can be weapons of mass destruction against forces of evil in the unseen realm. We've got a choice to make. "It's the righteous man who lives for the next generation," says Dennis Rainey of FamilyLife Ministries. "This is not the time for peace, it's time for war. Raise your kids to become arrows for war."[3] Only then will our kids be the conquerors God intended, not the casualties.

As Andrew Murray, one of the fathers of the faith, states in his book *Raising Your Children for Christ*, "Let us devote every child to God and His service. Let us stop praying that our children will be saved if we are not willing to offer them for His service. Let us lay each child upon the altar. Let us seek this one thing—that they may become worthy and equipped to be set apart for the service of the King. Let your example teach the Church that there are those who, because they love their children most intensely, know nothing better for them than to yield them to the will and the work of their God."[4]

Papa leads this kind of world-changer parenting by example. He's provided a roadmap for us of visionary parenting at its best—parenting that focuses less on what your family can do for God and more importantly on what God wants to do through your family.

Papa is not simply a visionary parent. I personally believe his purpose is much bigger than that. Leaving his homeland in south India to move 1,400 miles to an uncharted destination selected by God in north India, he has now become the father of a multitude of orphans who are currently blessing and changing their world for Christ. I believe Papa is truly *a modern day Abraham.*

How exciting is this? You and I can join Papa, raising our kids to be part of his vision of one million arrows for God. We are definitely in need of a great awakening in our country, and our families have more opportunity now than ever before to reach across neighborhoods, cities, states, and even borders to make a difference.

Someday, we are going to leave this world. Our kids are going to leave this world. Until then, what are we here for? Will we model for them fireman-like courage, raising them to leave behind that same kind of legacy for their children? Will we raise them to offer their lives—their time, talents, and resources—so that others can know Jesus? There's never been a better time to get started, because something is going down in history, and you're going to want to take part in it. *It's time to own the mission.*

CHAPTER 3

OWN THE MISSION

*But my life is worth nothing unless I use it for doing the work
assigned me by the Lord Jesus—the work of telling others the
Good News about God's wonderful kindness and love.*
                                                            —Acts 20:24

Find your passion and make it your ministry.
                                                            —Alvin Reid[1]

One of the most important days of our lives is the day when we realize *why
we were born.* The same goes for our kids.

For Ivan van Vuuren, that moment came when he was barely old
enough to carry a surf board. Now, every day when he throws his feet over
the side of the bed to go hit the waves, Ivan knows exactly why he was
born. Ivan is one of the world's most recognized all-around extreme sports
athletes and has won awards in surfing, windsurfing, and motocross racing.
Born in South Africa to missionaries, Ivan surrendered his life to Jesus as
an arrow at the age of five, and he has used his love of extreme sports ever

since then to tell others about Jesus. Now he's the International Director of Xtreme Life International, and president of Premier Productions, one of the world's leading extreme sports production companies. His ministry produces extreme sports movies with a Gospel message, and also produces and hosts the weekly TV show, "Xtreme Life TV."

Not only does he know exactly why he was put on this earth, Ivan is the epitome of living with passion while pursuing his God-assigned mission. Now an adult, he travels all over the world, hosting and performing at extreme sports events for youth. After the local events, he gathers all the athletes and spectators, and shares a bold, straightforward, Gospel message. He invites volunteers from local communities to the scene to help the kids get into a local body of believers. The heart of his message to kids is to get them into a relationship with Jesus so they can live with purpose:

> Over the years I've been fortunate to win many great things like cars and medals, attained fame and things that satisfy for the moment, but you know what? Nothing compares to that of living an XTREME LIFE for Christ! There might be times in your life when you feel like you can't go on and you want to quit your Christian walk or even quit at life. I want to encourage you to keep your eyes on the finish line and the prize of eternal life that awaits you.
>
> If you're tired of just "getting by" and you believe there must be more, and if questions like, "What am I here for?" and "What should I do with my life?" keep coming to your mind, it's a good time to sign up for the XTREME LIFE and to meet the most extreme Person who ever lived—Jesus Christ. No one has done, and no one will ever do what He has done for you. He loves you and has an amazing plan for your life! He forgives your sin and offers you eternal life if you believe and follow after Him. He's inviting you into the XTREME LIFE with Him. [2]

Some people think that you have to give up what you love to pursue God's plan for your life, but people like Ivan know that nothing could be further from the truth. He totally gets it that God made him to love certain things, and that he can be an arrow while being exactly the person God made him to be. His life motto, picked up when he was a kid trying to get up the courage to surf the huge waves off the coast of South Africa, and always his parting words to his audience: *"If you don't go, you'll never know."*

What Ivan is really all about is *the mission*—being Jesus to the world through his passions, abilities, and resources. *The mission* is not just about working as a full-time missionary, but about accepting a part of a bigger story where there is a battle being waged between lies and truth; between destruction and redemption; between darkness and light; between death and life, where ultimately goodness and love prevail. God has written an individual part for each of us in this story, and this part is our mission. It's a job for arrows because, without arrows, the battle cannot be won, and *the mission* cannot be accomplished.

Arrows and the Mission

When it comes to combat, what is the purpose of an arrow? Once a branch is gathered, it is honed, shaped, and then skillfully prepared to inflict a deadly wound against an enemy. Once launched, an arrow aims high and heads straight for a target, without getting off course. The ultimate goal for all arrows of God is that wherever they land, they produce mortal wounds against the Enemy of darkness—wounds of light, love, truth, and life. This is exactly the picture God had in mind when He referred to our children as arrows in the hands of a Warrior!

Being an arrow for *the mission* can look quite diverse for each person, because everyone has a different background, a unique shaping process, a different location where they will land, and a different impact, based on their gifts, abilities, training, and God's individual plan for them. But only those who accept *the mission* will fully discover what they were made to do on this earth.

What is *the mission?* "And the Good News about the Kingdom will be preached throughout the whole world, so that all nations will hear it; and then, finally, the end will come" (Matthew 24:14).

One million arrows invites individuals and families into *the mission* with people like Papa to take part in a great vision to finish the work of taking God's Good News to the people, tribes, and nations who still need to learn about Jesus (Revelation 7:9). In India alone, it is estimated that at least 80,000 people die every day without having heard the name of Jesus. What about the Americas? Asia? Africa?

It used to be that in order to spread the Gospel to other parts of the world, everyday people like you and me had to leave our homes and head to the mission field. But with the advances in communication, dynamics are changing. We can "preach" the Gospel in a variety of ways and from a variety of locations (we'll explore more on this later).

Papa sees this modern opportunity gaining momentum. "The Lord has opened a great and powerful door for believers in the last days—the door to preach in Russia, Romania, Korea, Hungary, China, Philippines, Africa, India, Nepal, and Burma," Papa says. "The door is also going to be opened in all the Islamic nations and in Israel, despite the opposition. Satan will try to stop this work, but God's plan for this world is greater than the plans of our adversary. He has asked us to enter the open door and preach the Gospel. When He opens this door, no one will be able to shut it" (Revelation 3:7).

If we want to follow Christ, we don't have a choice about engaging *the mission*, especially with our own little disciples at home. 1 John 2:6 says, "Whoever claims to live in Him must walk as Jesus did." This is what we're called to do, and to train our children to do. Only when *the mission* is complete will we finally get to settle in our real home, taking a permanent vacation from our problems, disappointments, and lost dreams. We'll be reunited with loved ones and one day live on a restored earth full of unimaginable beauty, nice people, uncorrupted justice, unending discoveries, and extreme adventure. Kind of motivating to get out there and tell everybody about Jesus, if you ask me.

The Result: Existing or Living?

God is ready to hand over the keys to each of His followers for a special assignment, but some of us rarely show up for the action, because we think it will either be boring or else it will cost too much. During my years in youth ministry, I couldn't believe how many kids admitted to me that they weren't ready to surrender to God's plan for them yet, because they weren't ready to "*give up their fun. Maybe later.*"

Where do we ever get the notion that following God's will for our lives is going to be boring and under-challenging? It certainly doesn't come from the Bible, history, or today's worthy examples. If you had the chance to ask any of the men and women throughout history who have demonstrated exemplary faith if they ever felt shorted in life by the difficulties they faced while pursuing *the mission*, or if they had regrets, I think you'd find a surprising yet comforting truth. The more challenging *the mission* became, the deeper their passion grew. The more their passion grew, the more willing for higher stakes they became. The more willing for higher stakes they became, the more God used them to do impossible things and the more their faith and passion in Him grew. It's a beautiful, self-perpetuating, irresistible process, this journey of faith. Frederick Buechner, one of America's foremost writers and theologians, once said, "The place God calls you to (your ministry) is the place where your deepest gladness and the world's deepest hunger meet."[3]

What's the alternative if we refuse? In his book, *Wild Goose Chase: Reclaim the Adventure of Pursuing God*, Mark Batterson reminds us: "I'm not convinced that your date of death is the date carved on your tombstone. Most people die long before that. We start dying when we have nothing worth living for."[4] Until we live for *the mission*, it can often feel that there's not much worth getting excited about. Sometimes it might even feel like there's not much worth living for.

This is exactly where Nick found himself. Nick Vujicic (pronounced voyi-chich) entered the world in Melbourne, Australia on December 4, 1982, with seemingly no abilities or future opportunities. He was born with no arms or legs. Despite the doctor's belief that baby Nick wouldn't survive for very long, tests came back that, other than no limbs, he was a perfectly healthy baby. Understandably, Nick's parents, who served in Christian ministry, were devastated. "If God is a God of love," they questioned, "then why would He let something like this happen, and especially to committed Christians?"[5]

As he entered school bound to a wheelchair, Nick tried to be like other kids, but it was impossible. Feeling the sting of rejection when teased and bullied by classmates, anger and depression overwhelmed him at times. "I still got hung up on the fact that, if God really loved me, why did He make me like this?" Convinced he was a burden to those around him, and believing there could be no valuable purpose for a twelve-year-old in his condition, he toyed with the idea of suicide. Thankfully, through the love and support of his family, Nick made a turnaround, and began to realize that God wanted him to use the hurts and disappointments of his circumstances to help others.

At fifteen, Nick fully turned his life over to Christ, while reading John 9. In this chapter, Jesus said that the reason a certain man was born blind was "so that the power of God could be seen in him" (vs. 3). With his incredible disability, Nick realized he could become a great opportunity for and testimony of God's awesome power. Since then, his life has become just that. God has given him spectacular opportunities that others would never dream of. Like the time his plane was delayed pulling into the gate after landing, and he shuffled out of his seat and into the aisle of the plane to share Christ, commanding the attention of everyone on board, including the flight crew. They were too flabbergasted to stop him.

"God began to instill a passion of sharing my story and experiences to help others cope with whatever challenge they might have in their lives . . . and I found my purpose! The Lord is going to use me to encourage and inspire others to live to their fullest potential and not let anything get in the way of accomplishing their hopes and dreams."[6]

To this day, Nick believes that nothing about his life can be attributed to bad luck or chance; it all happened in order to reveal Jesus to the world through him. Now in his mid-twenties, he travels worldwide as an inspirational speaker, encouraging his listeners, especially teens, that God has a great purpose for their lives, no matter what.

Nick is just one story of so many young people feeling worthless. With all the brokenness, aimlessness, and boredom among today's youth, it's apparent that they, as much as ever, display a certain need for speed. I believe this innate quality is a God-given thirst. Our kids want more passion. They want more risk. They crave significance. Even in Bible days, kids were given big assignments full of exciting challenges, daring adventures, human impossibilities, and even death-defying feats. And if we parents are willing to grasp and live in *the mission* ourselves, we'll understand the passion it can bring to our whole family.

Go for Goose Bumps

Mark Batterson likens this satisfying pursuit of God and His plan for our lives to a Wild Goose chase (hence the name of his book). "Pursuing our passions is the key to living a fruitful and fulfilling life. It is the thing that wakes us up early in the morning and keeps us up late at night. It is the thing that turns a career into a calling. It is the thing that gives us goose bumps—Wild Goose bumps. And nothing will bring you greater joy."[7]

Kohl Crecelius came down with a case of Holy Goose bumps when he began using his passion for *crocheting* to impact the world. Understand, Kohl is not some wimpy guy. He's actually a surfer and snowboarder dude who got started crocheting when his older brother, Parc, came home from college and introduced him to this newfound craft he used to relieve tension at school. Kohl started crocheting beanies (trendy caps) with a couple of his friends, and got "hooked." Eventually, it turned into a nice little side business when they started receiving orders at school.

During college summers, Kohl and his two buddies went on separate mission trips to different parts of the world. One of his friends came back from Uganda, deeply moved by the poverty and hopelessness of the Ugandan women.

Eventually, Kohl got the idea to teach these women how to crochet the beanies in order to earn a living, so he started the non-profit company, Krochet Kids International. "The idea behind Krochet Kids," Kohl said, "is to equip women in poor countries with a functional skill that allows them to make and sell items in their local communities. Krochet Kids supplies the women with the raw materials, tools and training, and pays them a base wage for their efforts. The organization also sells the handmade products in the U.S., raising additional funds to be sent back to the craftswomen's communities."

Kohl made a special trip to Uganda with friends to teach the young women—mostly mothers in their teens and early twenties—how to crochet, and they picked up the craft right away. Recently a graduate from college in international business, a twenty-something Kohl is moving forward with the company. "It's definitely pretty comical to think about, some college-age guys crocheting with some crazy idea of changing the world," said Kohl. "But maybe it's so unique and different, it actually works."[8]

Notice that many of these people pursuing *the mission* began making a difference while they were still youngsters. Alex and Brett Harris, Ivan, Nick, and now Kohl were all kids when God began using them in mighty ways. I've noticed this pattern throughout history. It wasn't typically the powerful and important people born into opportunity that God used for His community-impacting, culture-revolutionizing, world-changing plans. It was frequently the simple, overlooked, willing—often times *kids*!

While education, opportunities, and even abilities are great, they're not prerequisites for becoming one of God's world-changers!

This is good news for parents, and it's good news for people like Papa who are investing in broken and abandoned children worldwide. There are many reminders throughout the Bible of young people, many with seemingly no chance at a future, bringing about change in the world. One orphan girl was put in position to use her God-given beauty to save her Jewish people in 127 countries from annihilation (Esther 4:16–17). One teenager, initially left for dead by his own brothers in an abandoned well, used His God-given gifts of interpreting dreams and asserting leadership to save a whole nation from a deadly seven-year famine (Joseph, Genesis 30–47). One man's humility and passion for justice was used to deliver a whole nation (millions) from crushing slavery in Egypt into the Promised Land of abundance, liberty, and rest from their enemies (Moses, Exodus and Numbers). Another young man, the weakest in all of Israel, was divinely transformed into a powerful warrior to destroy an entire valley swarming with bloodthirsty warriors (Gideon, Judges 6:14–16).

The world is waiting for the Esthers, Josephs, Moseses, and Gideons to rescue them out of their enslavement to sin, spiritual sickness, ignorance, fear, demonic oppression, hatred, and death. Future great leaders like these sit abandoned in the death wells of poverty in cities and villages worldwide, waiting to be rescued so they can become God's great saviors of nations.

And others sit in your living room every night, unaware without your guidance that a crucial, life-saving mission is waiting—one tailored just for them.

Times Are Ripe

That's really what *the mission* is all about—being Jesus to the hurting, empty, hopeless world in your own individual way. It's really not about us. We've been called beyond ourselves for something bigger.

Craig Gross starts every day feeling the urgency and sheer magnitude of this "something bigger." In 2002, he started a website, XXXChurch.com, primarily as a resource for Christians struggling with pornography. In a nonscientific poll he conducted, 70 percent of *Christian* men admitted to struggling with porn in their *daily* lives. A whopping 76 percent of pastors surveyed admitted to struggling with porn at some level.[9] Craig began to offer free porn accountability software on the website, which has now been downloaded by over 500,000 visitors.

Eventually, Craig felt it was time to expand his reach to the unbelievers. He was struck by the realization that missionaries had boldly gone where few were willing to go, but the homeland industry of pornography was still among uncharted territory. Soon after, he and his co-worker, J.R. Mahon, began attending porn conventions, especially the annual "Adult Expo" in Las Vegas, handing out Bibles inscribed with, "Jesus Loves Porn Stars." The two men hope that in giving out free Bibles, someone will read one, desiring to seek truth and make a lifestyle change. "The Bible says the Word won't return void," says J.R. "I prayed as I unloaded those Bibles in the booth before anyone got here, 'God do a miracle in these people's lives.'"[10]

Craig and J.R. also spend time talking with any and all curious passersby about God's love for them. They adamantly believe that they are just obeying Jesus' commandment. "We've got to meet people where they're at. That's the Great Commission," says Craig. "I think that God is using people that work with XXXChurch.com to carry out His plan."[11]

It's stories like these that inspire me. Maybe it's the edginess of this unique calling that these young men are willing to pursue, despite heated criticism they receive from certain "Christians." But one thing's for sure. Their God-appointed purpose is something they're passionate about, and they're truly making an impact in many lives devastated by this gripping sin.

I can totally see Jesus standing at the Las Vegas Expo, telling the empty, hurting, enslaved people, "I have a plan for you. I died for you so that you could get free of this lifestyle because *I love porn stars*. Come away with me, and let me heal your empty soul for good."

As you can see from our examples, there are so many ways that people are living out *the mission* in their daily lives. Relinquishing our kids to become God's arrows does not necessarily mean they will all end up living in jungles with savages. God has many uses for our kids' abilities in His Kingdom work. But you can be sure that, once they've made the decision to be arrows, the direction they're aimed will be an exact match with their gifts, desires, and personalities—even if they haven't fully discovered them yet.

Will we face this call with excitement and courage? Or will we shrink away in fear, missing out on the Wild Goose bumps?

"You know what is most lacking?" Mark Batterson asks. "Good old-fashioned guts! We need people who are more afraid of missing opportunities than making mistakes. People who are more afraid of lifelong regrets than temporary failure. People who dare to dream the unthinkable and attempt the impossible."[12]

Sure, it will take a good dose of guts and even some imagination to take part in such a divine calling with our families. Some of our children may be called eventually to go to the mission field as arrows, either in their own country or somewhere else, for either short-term or long-term mission work. Others will use their talents, finances, prayers, or vocations to help support the ones who are called to go. They will have the equally important mission of sending arrows, which we will discuss later.

We are living in ripe times for *the mission* to be accomplished—finished! Never before have we had the technology, the mobility, the communication, and the opportunities we do now. If we all join together, there's no reason we cannot work toward making this a reality in our time. The sooner we make Him known throughout the world, the sooner we all get to go home—the sooner we get a permanent vacation. Sounds like heaven to me.

Now it's time to get started with the shaping process. As we embark on this wonderful and, at times, perilous adventure, I want to introduce you to a man who will help us recognize one of the greatest threats to a family's future potential as arrows for God.

PART 2
SHARPEN

Listen, far-flung islands,

pay attention, faraway people:

God put me to work from the day I was born.

The moment I entered the world He named me.

He made me His straight arrow and hid me in His quiver.

He said to me, "You're my dear servant,

through whom I'll shine."

Yes, God took me in hand from the moment of

birth to be His servant,

to bring His people back home to Him.

What an honor for me in God's eyes!

And now He says, "But that's not a big enough job

for my servant—

just to recover your own family, merely to round up

the strays of your own people.

I'm setting you up as a light for the nations

so that my salvation becomes global!"

—Paraphrased from Isaiah 49:1–6, MSG

CHAPTER 4

GATHER BROKEN
BRANCHES

*Remain in me, and I will remain in you. For a branch cannot
produce fruit if it is severed from the vine, and you cannot be
fruitful apart from me.*

—John 15:4

*Even before we think of it, weakness can become wickedness in
ourselves and our children.*

—Andrew Murray[1]

As 35-year-old James Kim set out for home with his family in November
2006 after a holiday vacation in the Pacific Northwest, there's a good
chance he was thinking primarily about meeting the immediate needs
and best interests of his young family when he opted to take the shortcut
through the Klamath Mountains. His two daughters, ages four years and
seven months, were perhaps restless and fussy in their car seats. His wife
was likely worn out from traveling with needy kids. Everyone was probably

ready to get home as soon as possible, and James was only doing what he thought best to take care of his travel-weary family.

The Kims didn't make it across the mountains that day because James apparently didn't realize that the road was impassible. When their car became snowbound, they were stuck in the middle of nowhere with few emergency supplies, no cell service, and no way out. The family tried waiting it out for a whole week, staying with the car, making do to survive with what they had. Finally, out of desperation, James left his family, traveling by foot for seven miles in search of help, a heroic move that cost him his life. Rescuers later said he was so dogged in his determination to save his family, that they were not even able to follow his trail in places through areas of difficult and treacherous terrain. Thankfully, the rest of the family was found and rescued in the nick of time.

According to those who knew him, James was no stranger to the ways of the mountains. In fact, if anyone should have been able to help his family to safety, it was this experienced and capable man. Andrea Macari, a friend and clinical psychologist noted, "He had the determination of a father and a husband. He loved the outdoors. He was sort of like a closeted mountain man of a sort. He camped. He had lived in Oregon before. And he was also this gadget geek. He had the savvyness, the sophistication. You really would have thought he would have been able to navigate his way out of this one."[2]

If James was really that on top of it, there's a chance he knew he was making a risky choice by heading for the mountain route. Part of him knew the safest route home, but too caught up in momentary gain or shortsighted ease, he failed to take it.

As I heard that story, I couldn't help but wonder, *how many of us are like James?* The love we have for our families defies description. We would do anything to make life the easiest, greatest, and most fun for them, to protect them, and to watch out for their best interests. Without a doubt we, like James, would give our very lives for them.

But what if—we find out too late—we've taken too big of a risk, putting our family in danger? Perhaps somewhere along the way we tried to take a shortcut, settling for an easier route in the spiritual development of our children by relying too heavily on someone else to do the work, and now we find that they needed more than a couple hours of spiritual training a week. Now we find that our determined love and best of intentions alone aren't enough to arrive safely "home." How can we know for sure?

Evidence of Danger

Maybe you don't know what I'm talking about. As far as you can tell, your kids are doing just fine, thriving spiritually with few major concerns. That could be true for your kids, but when it comes to *most Christian kids*, there is reason to be very concerned. The faith of many of our kids has become fragile, brittle, even broken and dying, much like branches without enough pruning, or branches subjected to harsh elements without proper protection and nutrients.

As someone who worked in Christian youth ministry for twelve years, I learned firsthand about what some of our kids are dealing with on a regular basis—from gripping temptations to appallingly immoral scenes at school. Many of them, along with their close friends, frequently battle anxiety, boredom, purposelessness, depression, and temptation toward life-shattering sins. They rub shoulders with kids (and teachers) at school who are sexually active, sexually disoriented, abusing drugs, and even contemplating suicide. My own girls encountered these kinds of situations at school as early as sixth grade, and that while growing up in fairly sheltered, small town America. On top of that, our kids hear about students who suddenly go on killing sprees, wondering if it will happen at their school, too. Many of our own kids are not only far from thriving in this environment; they're barely surviving.

I've encountered many kids from nice Christian families, great youth groups, and even Christian schools who care very little about God's plan for their future, setting goals, family relationships, obeying authority, and seeking out a personal, dynamic relationship with God. To fill their need-for-speed, many of our kids bury themselves in gaming, social networking, TV and reality shows, graphic movies, and other forms of mind-numbing amusement, often at the expense of meaningful family relationships or selfless contributions in the lives of others. Our little ones grow up having almost everything their hearts desire, yet for so many, their hearts are still beyond empty. Their faith does not seem to be the anchor that holds on the rough seas of life.

Think I'm exaggerating? The statistics tell us that currently, three out of every four Christian young people are leaving church for good by their second year in college.[3] 85 percent of our own "born again teens" do not believe in the existence of absolute truth, and more than half of those surveyed actually believe that Jesus sinned during his earthly life.[4]

It appears that the firemen are fast becoming the victims. The impact of modern culture has put the spiritual survival of our children at stake!

In his book, *Battle Cry for a Generation: The Fight to Save America's Youth*, Ron Luce of Teen Mania Ministries implores parents and ministry leaders to take a serious look at the spiritual poverty of our nation's young people—our own broken branches—before it's too late.

"People, the car is on fire and the youth of America are trapped inside. The stakes are staggering—we have in America today 33 million teenagers, the largest group of teens since World War II. This generation of youth has the potential to impact our nation—economically, politically, spiritually—with every bit as much force as the Baby Boomers have. These young people are our sons and daughters, grandsons and granddaughters, nieces and nephews. They are the future of America. We've got to get them out [of the burning car]—whatever it takes—we've got to get them out."[5]

This can't be, we shake our heads in disbelief. Our children are in church on Sunday, and in youth programs during the week. They attend summer church camps and youth rallies. It seems they have far more op-portunities to grow in their faith now than when we were kids, right?

One concerned educator and youth ministry expert, Alvin Reid, author of *Raising the Bar: Ministry to Youth in the New Millennium*, shares his observation: "For the past three decades . . . youth ministry has exploded across America, accompanied by a rise in the number of degrees in youth ministry granted by colleges and seminaries, an abundance of books and other resources, and a network of cottage industries devoted solely to youth ministry. Yet those same three decades have failed to produce a generation of young people who graduate from high school or leave youth groups ready to change the world for Christ."[6] Add to that, Reid notes that our churches are in fact showing a startling decline of youth ministry effectiveness.[7]

Let me reassure you that this is not the fault of youth ministries. Many are doing their best to teach our kids through excellent programs and opportunities. Surely without their tireless devotion to the spiritual growth of our children, we would see even more casualties.

So what is the problem? What is the missing link in the spiritual vitality of our children?

Well-known researcher George Barna, author of *Revolutionary Parenting*, reveals part of the answer after interviewing thousands of families over a quarter of a century: *"Churches alone do not and cannot have much influence on children"* (emphasis mine).[8] He elaborates, "The responsibility for raising spiritual champions (believers who continually seek to deepen their relationship with God, impact others for Christ, and accept the Bible as authoritative truth), according to the Bible, belongs to parents. The spiritual nurture of children is supposed to take place in the home. Organizations and people from outside the home might support those efforts, but the responsibility is squarely laid at the feet of the family. This is not a job for specialists. It is a job for parents."[9]

Wow. That puts a new spin on modern-day parenting. When I grew up, it was the youth pastor's job to evangelize and disciple kids, and even to engage them in the needs of the world. But now it's clearer than ever that it's not the youth pastor's job. It's mine. It's yours. Voddie Baucham

(Family Driven Faith) says, "The [faith] retention rate is not highest among those in youth groups; it is highest among those whose parents (particularly fathers) disciple them. Ask any youth pastor and he'll tell you. The kids who stay [committed] are the ones whose parents are investing in them."[10]

So that's what it means to "take the long way home." Making it a priority to begin investing spiritually in our children at home, and not depending on anyone else to get the job done right. Along with the statistics, let's look at some more convincing reasons why this is exactly the route we as parents want to choose.

Battle for the Souls: a Godless Generation

Judges 2:10 will likely disturb any parent who sincerely wants to raise God-revering, world-changing kids. "After that generation died, another generation grew up who did not acknowledge the LORD or remember the mighty things he had done for Israel."

With the current reality of our kids' faith revealing itself to be more skin deep than soul deep, a godless generation is a horribly shocking, imminent possibility looming on our horizon. There seems to be one anti-dote, a common theme throughout the Old Testament. My favorite version is located in Psalm 78:4–8 (selected): "We will not hide these truths from our children but will tell the next generation about the glorious deeds of the LORD. We will tell of his power and the mighty miracles he did. For he issued his decree . . . He commanded our ancestors to teach them to their children, so the next generation might know them—even the children not yet born—that they in turn might teach their children. So each generation can set its hope anew on God, remembering his glorious miracles and obeying his commands. Then they will not be like their ancestors—stubborn, rebellious, and unfaithful, refusing to give their hearts to God."

Well-known speaker, author, and apologist (defender of faith), Josh McDowell, has a passion for helping parents reclaim their God-given role as the spiritual leaders of their children. In his book, *The Last Christian Generation*, he opens with this sentence: "I sincerely believe unless something is done now to change the spiritual state of our young people—*you [parents] will become the last Christian generation!*" (emphasis mine).[11]

Are we willing to sit and watch, indifferent to the fact that we parents very well could become the last Christian generation, and our children could become the immediate generation that doesn't remember our God?

The way I see it, our kids can rise above difficult circumstances. They can overcome the moral and ethical decline of their cultural environment. They can fight off the constant in-your-face temptations of their generation. But what can never be overcome are continued and deliberate shortcuts taken by those entrusted to bring them safely home. Let history bear the proof.

What's sad to me is this: even when confronted with the warning that we're heading the wrong way—that life-threatening dangers lay down the easier, shorter road, or that we have already lost our way and are putting our kids' spiritual futures at stake—many Christian parents do not care enough to change their ways.

While submitting this book to publishers for consideration, I received a rejection letter from an editor who works for a prominent Christian family ministry and publishing house that interacts with hundreds of thousands of Christian parents each year. He told me that he loved the concept of this book, but there was one little problem. While parents heartily express that the spiritual training of their kids is their top priority, they seldom follow through on that priority when given opportunities "in real life." He also informed me, based on this particular ministry's experience, they agree with The Barna Group's statistical findings that today's Christian parents: generally rely upon their church to do most, if not all, of their children's religious training; they have no plan for the spiritual development of their children; they do not consider it a priority in their own homes and daily lives; and they don't typically have any spiritual goals for their families.[12] The Barna findings go on to report that the parents who were interviewed tend to fall back on a survival-based approach to parenting at home (i.e. put out destructive fires started by your kids) rather than a goal-oriented approach (i.e. start world-changing fires with your kids).[13]

The fact is, many of us know the road we need to take, or at least we have access to the right maps and road reports, but too often we're looking for shortcuts—a way out of the longer, seemingly harder road of raising our kids with an eternal perspective and a biblical worldview.

Do we care enough to stop this cycle before it's too late?

A Holy Calling

God chose you to be the parent of your children. He gave you the vote of confidence that there is no one better suited in this whole world for the job of raising your kids to love Him wholeheartedly and to keep the faith.

That's exactly the conclusion Bart Pierce came to in the late 90s. Bart is the senior pastor of Rock City Church in Baltimore, Maryland. Until that time, RCC had gone all out with youth programs to raise up the next generation of spiritual leaders. They had a K–12 Christian school with chapel services, a dynamic Friday night youth group meeting, and many other programs and activities geared totally to the kids. Says Bart, "We didn't do 'average' with our kids because we were investing in them."[14]

As these same kids grew up and went off to college, the church leaders noticed a troubling trend. The kids did fine spiritually while connected to the church, but when they went off to college, the majority of them veered off course. Bart realized they weren't doing something right and it bothered him. "After that I began to notice how many youth pastors burn out. I looked at those pieces [of the puzzle] and I thought, maybe we're putting pressure on those youth pastors that they never were called to take on. There's no way they have enough grace to raise someone else's kids."

Around that time, Bart felt strongly that the Lord impressed upon him that the church had taken the place of the parents. "We had taken the children from the parents, attempting to give these kids their values and their spiritual direction. This left the parents unmotivated, letting us do the work for them."

So Bart called all the parents together at the church one Friday night. In front of a wide-eyed, incredulous crowd, he spoke, "Okay, I repent for trying to take your place with your children. We are missing the mark. I give you your children back tonight."

"What am I going to do with my kids on Friday nights?" many parents lamented. And Bart said, "That's my point. I'm giving your kids back because I want you to train them." Bart challenged parents to think about the big picture and what Christianity would look like a few years down the road if they didn't start taking responsibility to train their kids at home. "What will the church look like in ten or twelve years? We'll have kids who step out of church and don't go back; we'll have kids who don't know how to tithe because they were never taught to do that. They won't know how to pray. They'll never read books or the Bible. The next generation of Christians is not going to be a healthy generation."

At that point, Bart made a bold move. He put an end to the weekly youth groups, and he rearranged the Christian school to end at fifth grade, encouraging parents to begin spending time with their kids at home talking about morals, about matters of faith, and about how to be a witness for Christ. But he also made an extremely wise decision that ended up teaching the kids how to mature and serve, rather than always being catered to. He opened up all the ministries of the church, and any youth twelve years or older could be mentored and taught to serve in any ministry of his or her choice. Worship, music, video recording, and community projects—all were open to the kids.

How have they fared? "I'll tell you the truth," Bart beams with pride. "I never noticed a difference when the kids were running camera or when skilled adults were."

Since all these changes have been made, the church has had enough years to track the trend of their post high school kids. The church dropout trend has been reversed, and the kids have generally taken ownership of their faith, thriving in college and beyond.

You and I can learn from this example. We have a very short window of time on this earth to impact our children's lives for eternity and to make sure they don't go through their days unequipped to answer the questions they'll likely wrestle with as they approach adulthood: *Why am I here? What is my purpose? Where am I going? How do I get there? What does the future hold?* We can no longer afford to stand by, watching them succumb to the devastating lies of the devil and the world, but instead we must be ready to give them what their hearts are deeply longing for: an authentic relationship with their Creator, living out the purpose He created them for in the big picture. I believe our kids are not looking for the easy road; they're looking for the eternal road.

U-Turn for Home

Maybe you agree so far, but you feel the crushing fear that you're too late. I have to admit that after reading what other parents are doing to beat the odds (things I never thought of doing), and now that my own girls are practically grown, I was tempted to swallow this lie, especially with my limited time spent with them through divorce custody sharing. But God has shown me over and over that first and foremost, He is ultimately in control. He alone can direct the outcome of His children's lives. There are so many examples of this throughout the Bible, throughout history, as well as in our world today.

Take for instance, Patrick McDonald of Denmark. He was just five years old when a drunk driver killed his older brother. Next, he watched his mother sink into deep depression that robbed him of a meaningful relationship with her during his childhood. Then, when he turned twelve, his dad suddenly died from cancer. With raw, inconsolable grief at this final blow, he bolted into the woods behind his house, running until he tripped and fell, exhausted. On the forest floor, he sobbed with his head to the ground, "God, if you're there, please be my dad." Patrick was unprepared for what came next. He still remembers as if it happened yesterday: "It felt as if Jesus picked me up and gave me a hug."

This supernatural experience with the "Father to the fatherless" (Psalm 68:5) was a turning point spiritually for Patrick. He surrendered his life to God, and five years later, at seventeen, he went to Bolivia (South America) to work with street kids. There he cried out to God in frustration over the great chasm between God's mandate to help suffering children and the stark reality of life for so many on the streets. And once again, God reached perceptibly into his world, only this time with words spoken to his heart. "I'm as frustrated as you are, Patrick. It's terrible! But are you willing to help me do something about it?"

About that time, God gave Patrick a vision of starting the ministry Viva Network, a cooperative movement of Christians passionately concerned for children at risk. In order to begin this ministry, Patrick spent every last penny of his inheritance from his father, but in the end it paid off. *Viva* has developed into a global network, with eighty-one initiatives in forty-eight countries, providing for well over a million children.

"We create networks among Christians caring for children," Patrick explains, "because collaboration brings greater effectiveness. Our aim is to map the whole world of Christian care for children by 2014. We believe it will cause a revolution by empowering connections, preventing duplication, and identifying need."

In spite of the spiritual and parental deficiencies of Patrick's childhood, God ultimately led him into a life-changing relationship and meaningful, world-impacting future. But having said that, we're not exactly off the hook either; God will still hold us responsible *for what we know*. But He is, most thankfully, a redeeming God and the God of second chances. With Him, it's never too late for change. Period. We can begin at anytime and at any age to influence our children in meaningful, eternal ways, and we don't have to do it alone. From the help of others who have gone before, we're about to discover many spiritual training ideas that can still make a difference for our children from now on so they can be launched from our homes as arrows (or ballistic missiles) aimed at the kingdom of darkness.

I believe that if you and I will start today, God will let us partner with Him to make up for lost time. And even as our kids become grown, we're not done with our responsibility for investing in His children. There are other kids throughout the world that He has given us the opportunity to invest in (we'll discuss more later), and there are always grandkids down the road who will need to be discipled in our faith as well.

Though there's certainly a lot at stake individually, there's also a lot at stake in the big picture. I believe our children are not just the future of America. With the great spiritual, financial, and educational opportunities available, I believe our kids have the opportunity to impact the spiritual future of the world. We as parents hold the keys to the opportunities and resources to make it possible.

So what's next? How do we raise our kids for *the mission?* Thankfully we have the examples of some seasoned pros who can help get us on our way.

CHAPTER 5

SHAPE ARROWS AT HOME

Teach your children to choose the right path, and when they are older, they will remain upon it.

—Proverbs 22:6

A child's training can decide what his life is to be.

—Andrew Murray[1]

Maybe you've heard of the "New Superman."

Tim Tebow is a modern-day legend. The first college underclassman to win the Heisman Trophy in its 73-year history (December 2007), Tim's athletic prowess includes two conference championships and two national championships. Rumor even has it around *Metropolis* that Superman has been seen wearing Tim Tebow pajamas. And while Tim is a football phenomenon, that's not even close to the most impressive thing about him. If you ask him how important football is to him, keeping in mind all the attention it brings from blood-thirsty cameras and sexy college girls asking him to autograph their underwear, Tim will tell you football is right up there at *number four,* right after God, family, and then academics. How does a young guy in this limelight of stardom keep his priorities straight? How does he keep from getting full of himself? How does he fight off testimony-crippling temptations that other college guys would consider fantastic opportunities?

"There's more important things in life than winning football games and going out and having fun," Tim says. "Everything I do, I'm trying to do the most important thing—like what's going to last for eternity. I don't want to be one of those guys who is looked at as just a football player. I want to be looked at as someone who is kind, and who treated others the way he wanted to be treated, and always tried to do the right thing. When it's all said and done, people aren't going to remember how many championships you won, they're going to remember what you were like off the field—how you treated people. My ultimate goal is not three championship rings. When God asks me what I did to help others, I can give him more than three championship rings."[2]

Pretty mature and amazing thought processes for one so young. The awesome thing is that Tim is only one of five kids in his family with the same priorities in life. It's obvious that he's the product of extraordinary parenting. What's the Tebows' secret?

Tim had parents who stuck to the safer, long way home by committing themselves to raising arrows. According to Tim, "I had a strong family who put the right priorities in front of me while I was young—a dad who put character in front of me and lived it out daily and a mom who taught me Scripture verses every day."[3]

The fact is, Bob and Pam Tebow didn't raise their son Tim to be a hero on the football field. They raised their son to be a hero on the field of life. "You can be well-educated in the world's eyes and still be a sorry person," Bob Tebow says. "You can graduate with degrees and have no character."[4] Tim's parents made decisions based on the big picture, not on immediate gratification, easy shortcuts, or personal comfort. From the beginning, they set out to raise kids who would make a lasting impact on this world.

"If I could get my kids to the age of twenty-five knowing and serving God, and having character qualities that please God, then I knew God would be happy and I would be happy," Bob says. "The only way I could do that was to *do it myself*—commit to God that this is *my job*."[5] For the Tebows, home schooling was the vehicle they chose for their job of shaping arrows. Most of their kids' life lessons began on their forty-four acre farm near Jacksonville, Florida, where traditional education took a back seat to learning God's Word and building character through their everyday lives.

When the Tebows realized how gifted Tim was at football, they saw a special opportunity. "Our goals weren't just typical goals," Bob says. "I tried to give him a vision early that if he worked hard and became a successful quarterback, he would have an amazing platform for Christ. Now he gets so many invitations [to speak] I don't even begin to keep track of them."[6]

What principles guided the Tebow household? A few they focused on were:

- Start training when they are young.
- Teach them to memorize Scripture.
- Emphasize humility and character above immediate pleasure and self-gratification.
- Teach them to give thanks to the Lord in everything.
- Use smaller problems to teach them how to deal with the bigger ones successfully.
- Teach them hard work in helping out around the home.
- Teach them not to praise or talk about themselves but to let others do it (the Tebows even discourage Tim from reading his own press clippings).
- Encourage them to pick heroes who model good character traits, such as humility.
- Get them outside of themselves from an early age, caring about the needs and problems of others.[7]

Practically speaking, the Tebows gave their kids lots of opportunities to grow in character throughout their childhood. The family always believed that getting their kids to focus on others by getting involved in *the mission* was a huge priority. A large part of their training field was a ministry they started in the Philippines, which is still in operation. The ministry includes an orphanage, much like Papa's, that brings up kids to make a spiritual difference in their own country. Every year the family returns to the Philippines to lead evangelistic outreaches; to visit prisons, hospitals, local churches; and to help out at the orphanage. The orphans don't know Tim as a football star, only as a regular guy who talks to and plays with them. During one trip his mom estimates that Tim had opportunities to speak to more than 30,000 people about his faith.[8]

"Tim's life is not totally wrapped up in football or awards," Pam says. "We have a lot of things going on that are more important in the scheme of life."[9]

Overall, the Tebows welcome the attention given to Tim, because they trust him to use that attention to get a more important message out. They believe God has allowed this opportunity for Tim because there's a bigger purpose in it all.

Raising arrows isn't just another formula to follow or another list of to-dos. It's a mentality, a *lifestyle,* and a *change of priorities* that permeates the whole family's lives and schedules, centering everyone on God's priorities and plans. It's rejecting the status quo of settling into the patterns of this world (Romans 12:1–2) and asking ourselves every day, "How can my family glorify God *today*? How can we train our kids to think about living for the big picture and not just for the here and now? How can we live for others instead of being out for ourselves?" And most importantly, "How can I be the spiritual leader my children need today?"

Samuel Thomas

Papa's son, Samuel, has been living away from his family by no choice of his own for about three years now. Because of serious persecution issues in India against his and many other Christian ministries, certain anti-Christians have threatened to kill his sons, so his family has relocated to the United States for safety. At the same time, the government has hardly permitted him to leave India to see them (only once or twice a year). Sam once shared with me, "One of my sons, Tim, is ten. When I'm away from my family, I email them devotions every day. Tim tells me, 'I love those devotions you send to us. You make the Bible so real to us.'

"My sons go to a Christian school, but I cannot depend on that Christian school for my children's spiritual education. If I want them to be where God wants them to be, I better invest in them. I can't wait for their youth pastor, or for the school staff.

"Most people pay attention to teaching adults. But it's the kids that bring you a clean slate. Changing your community and eventually the world starts with the home, teaching and training our kids, each and every day."

Josh McDowell

When Josh talks to parents at the seminars he conducts nationwide, he addresses the vital need of helping our kids find authentic, rational faith in an age when their peers and authority figures are not only skeptics, but also antagonists. Josh has a great array of family faith-building, culture-combating resources, some of which are listed in the resources at the end of this book.

I recently attended one of his seminars where he addressed the importance of competent influence by parents. "If you raise your kids [spiritually] the way you were raised, you'll lose them in today's world. They won't survive with the belief system you and I were raised with."[10]

The belief system he's referring to? The notion we were raised with that "faith is blind," and that one must accept biblical teachings without questioning the logical or historical reasoning behind it. Basically, Josh expresses two things that are driving away today's Christian youth from their spiritual heritage:

They don't experience it: Our kids need to experience authentic faith for themselves. Where does it start? With the parents. "You can't take your children further than you've gone yourself," Josh says. "When we're modeling true dependence on God with radical faith, and our kids can see the results, they will experience authentic Christianity. If it is real to us, it will be real to them."[11]

No one will answer their questions: Our kids' faith is constantly being challenged by an atheistic culture. As a result, they have tough questions that must be answered. Whether at school or through the media, they're bombarded daily by scoffers and doubt-planters. Josh contends that the "faith-is-blind-notion" is an outright lie. Our kids can and must learn rational, intelligent, factual answers to their toughest faith and history questions, and we must help them by seeking out answers for and with them. But before we can really impact our kids' lives, the first and foremost key to their hearts is through the *power of relationship*:

- Rules without *relationship* lead to rebellion.
- Truth without *relationship* leads to rejection.
- Discipline without *relationship* leads to bitterness.

"Relationships," Josh says, "are foundational to beliefs, values, and behavior. God doesn't work in a vacuum; He works through relationships. Jesus came to offer Himself in relationship with His people."[12] These days, relationships with our kids have been sacrificed to everyone's hectic schedules. But it doesn't have to be this way. We can reprioritize, making time to really connect with our kids, learning about their needs, desires, gifts, and abilities.

Lack of time is never a good excuse. If we say we are too busy to get to know and properly train our kids—the most precious responsibility we have been given on this earth—it's only a matter of misaligned priorities or self-deception. Everyone has the same number of hours, and there are many parents showing us how to reprioritize and make every minute of parenting count for eternity.

When we prioritize well, we'll teach our kids to do the same. Did you know that the typical preteen devotes on average more than forty hours per week ingesting media content?[13] We're to be the watchdogs over the family priorities and schedules because our kids aren't mature enough to figure out on their own what's truly important and beneficial. And many of them aren't learning any better by watching us! Even if we are raising kids alone, we can almost always arrange everyone's schedule so there's at least one or two hours a day for connecting and spiritual training.

One hour a day of focused time with your kids isn't much, but it's a great starting place. It adds up, too. Over a year, that's 365 hours, just over two weeks of training. Over eighteen years, that's 6,570 hours or thirty-nine weeks of training (more than two-thirds of a year). It's a great starting place that will make a significant difference—a difference that church and youth programs alone could never accomplish.

Gregg and Sono Harris

Remember our rebelutionaries, Alex and Brett, from Chapter Two? Meet the responsible party, Gregg and Sono Harris from Portland, Oregon, the proud managers of a name-brand "arrow factory." This couple has been raising arrows and teaching other parents how to do the same for over twenty-five years. They have four grown children, all doing their part to change the world, and three more still in the shaping process. Gregg, author of *The Christian Home School,* and pioneer in the international Christian homeschooling movement in the 80s and 90s, has definitely modeled arrow-mentality to his children.

Just like all our featured parents, the Harrises started their parenting journey with more questions than answers. But now, after so many years of on-the-job-training and successful results, they share some of the most important household practices that have worked for them:

Limit peer time: Proverbs 22:15 describes children as being foolish, and Proverbs 13:20 says, "Whoever walks with the wise will become wise; whoever walks with fools will suffer harm." From this concept, Gregg and Sono have derived that for their kids to spend too much time with age mates (outside of siblings) is, in effect, walking with fools. In order for children to become wise, they need to spend ample time with more mature and wiser people whom they can imitate in all the important areas of their lives—spiritual growth, communication, self-discipline, relationships, and personal development.

Including their kids significantly in their daily lives has been a large part of the Harrises parenting style, but this puts the demand on the parent to be the wise companion. They have to constantly prioritize and center on those things that are of eternal value. "For example," says Gregg, "you can be involved in great, life-impacting ministry, but if you don't include your children in that life, your ministry is over in one generation. On the other hand, you can be very inclusive with your kids but only use your time with them on recreation and time-wasters. Then, even though you have a good relationship, it doesn't have any direction."[14]

Consider homeschooling: Gregg and Sono believe the Christian homeschooling movement is an unrecognized revival in church history. If you feel that homeschooling isn't for you, the Harrises encourage you to take another look at what it really is, which is much more than just keeping your kids out of school. It has to do with pursuing a lifestyle of what Gregg calls *delight-directed study.* "When your kids are home in the evenings, or on the weekends, or in the summertime, you can make your home a center for study, instruction, and adventure. Eventually you may decide it's a waste of time to keep sending them to a conventional school that distracts them from the more effective and productive learning time at home."

The Harrises suggest investing in *tools* instead of *toys*, drawing your children into productive learning. As an example, they recently invested in a nice video camera for their thirteen-year-old so he can get involved in videography. It may be expensive, but they see it more as an investment—a tool. Since he's interested, learning this skill in depth will open doors for him. It will teach him how to become passionate about something and to learn how to study because he *wants* to know, rather than just to satisfy a school requirement.

"Let your kids learn to have fun at being productive, and then to purge the things in the home that function as 'mental junk food'—things that satisfy their boredom without delivering any benefit."

Find encouragement in opposition: Greg and Sono have learned that opposition doesn't always mean to back away. "We believe when you have a calling or clear direction from God, you have to take the opposition that comes along with it as evidence that you're on the right path." This goes along with what Paul said in 1 Corinthians 16:9, "A great door of opportunity has opened to me and there are many adversaries."

Gregg points out, "You know which door it is because there are all these big guys standing around it, trying to block you. We've found that by not giving up—persevering through opposition—you do reap along the way. You begin to see evidence of God's grace and blessing, and it gives you continued encouragement to keep going." This opposition might be in the form of resistance from your kids, criticism from others (maybe even believers) for your lifestyle choices, or financial obstacles.

Just say no: The Harrises believe parents should try to make decisions now that our children will thank us for when they're thirty, aiming at the big picture. Sometimes they feel sort of heavy handed with their kids, but they try not to be controlling. "We're big advocates of not just putting up fences to keep distractions out, but also building sidewalks so there are many opportunities for them to use their giftings now, and to use their time wisely in preparation for their future lives and ministries for the Kingdom of God. So there are a lot of yeses, too."

Saying no, even to *good* things, in order to pursue *best* things, must become a vigilant discipline for both parents and children alike. "We live in a world where, if you display any level of competence in any area, you'll have more opportunities to be busy than you can possibly respond to. So it's important to recognize the difference between an opportunity and a distraction, and to learn how to say no, while teaching your kids to say no as well. It's one of the hard things parents do, because your kids don't always see it at the time."

Since sheer willpower sometimes isn't enough, one giant "no" the Harrises decided upon was to television. All that extra time gave them the opportunity to read together as a family, and to pursue other activities and projects. "I've often said if you just harness boredom, it can pull your kids into a lot of exciting things as long as they don't have a lot of mental junk food around (time wasters, such as TV, texting, and internet surfing/ chatting) to destroy their appetite for being productive," Gregg says. "If they're busy with something they're excited about, that becomes a great alternative."

Go for the "greenhouse effect": A lot of parents, especially home-schooling parents, are criticized for being overprotective. But the Harrises describe parenting in terms of a greenhouse.

"When you want to have a strong crop in the future, you often have to start plants in a greenhouse, allowing them to get a good root system established. Ultimately, your goal is to transplant them to the field where they'll bear their fruit. But as they grow, that transition is a process. As they mature, you move them to a cold frame where they harden up and learn to handle the changing temperatures. They're no longer getting all the nurturing they were in the greenhouse, but neither are they exposed to the full force of the harsh winds and the elements.

"Young people, especially young adults, have more energy than they know what to do with. They're no longer children, and yet they don't have the responsibilities of their own family, and so it's important at that point that your household have a sense of vision and adventure in doing hard things for the glory of God. You don't want to *control* what they're doing, but you do want to *influence* what they're doing. You keep the communication loop small and frequent so that they have someone to talk to about what they're dealing with, providing counsel and encouragement, and maybe warnings if something's coming up that looks like it could be hazardous."

Gregg and Sono give God all the glory for stirring up their desire to invest in their kids so that they could become powerful arrows for God. Their family has become a team—an active partnership between the wisdom of the older members of the family and the energy of the younger members of the family.

Bill and Kristi Gaultiere

When Bill and Kristi Gaultiere of Irvine, California, were trying to decide how to raise their three children in the faith, they noticed that the Bible uses the word "Christian" only three times, but the word "disciple" occurs over 200 times. After careful study, they realized that a disciple of Christ is someone who is really serious about his faith, so they began looking for ways to raise *disciples*, not just Christians.

What exactly is discipleship? We mentioned earlier that it is teaching our children to live daily *with* Jesus, and to live *like* Jesus would have them live. It literally means "student" or "follower." When Jesus called out the twelve, He basically applied the parenting principles of Deuteronomy, especially chapter 11, in which parents are instructed to teach their children continuously in the course of life until His Word becomes etched in their hearts and minds, and His commandments become their constant guide in daily choices and life decisions.

Discipleship is in essence *training*, not just *teaching*. The parent who trains, first explains to the children what to do (teaches), then shows them by example how to do it (models), then follows through to make sure the children implement and practice the behavior (holds accountable). Only when we follow this model can our children truly be empowered to become disciples.

So as the Gaultieres committed to discipleship, they started with the usual stuff—attending church, praying with their kids at bedtime, and fellowshipping regularly as a family with other close-knit believers. But they also came up with three additional practices for their household that have made an amazing difference.

Work through the *Westminster Catechism*: The *Shorter Westminster Catechism* is a teaching tool that originated from the Reformation, intended to educate laypersons in the matters of doctrine and belief. In a simple question and answer format, it deals with such Biblical teachings as original sin, baptism, and communion. It is intended to lay the foundation for discipleship by teaching your children what to believe, but more importantly, *why*. One need not agree with every teaching in order to use it as a tool for educating and familiarizing your kids with the Bible. As a great alternative, I (Julie) have developed my own version (see the resources section) of the Catechism that is more contemporary and less denominational.

The Gaultieres begin this in-depth training with each of their children at age ten, slowly working through one question at a time, looking up Bible references, and discussing their findings together. This process actually takes about two years, working through the questions a little each night, until they feel that their kids really have a grasp on the basics.

Kristi says, "We implemented this teaching method when we recognized that there was a real gap they weren't getting filled at church or in Sunday school. Their need was to really understand the basic tenets of the Christian faith and what the Bible says."[15]

Walk them through the Bible: There's only one way to get the Word of God into your kids and that is to get your kids into the Word. One of the ways the Gaultieres facilitate this is to purchase a wide-margin Bible for each of their kids. Bill takes a year or two, prayerfully reading through, cover-to-cover, and little by little he writes prayers and notes containing special insights or application, with that particular child in mind.

Another important aspect of this for the Gaultieres is living out the Deuteronomy 6 passage, bringing up spiritual conversations as they go along in life—in a natural way—talking about the Lord while asking their kids questions and drawing out insights from everyday life.

Lastly, when they were frustrated with the selection of family devotionals on the bookstore shelves, Bill came up with his own simple but effective method. He picked out 365 verses, one for each day of the year, and put them into a three-ring binder. Each verse was simple and short, yet was tied to a crucial principle for being a disciple of Christ. You can also choose themes for each month, if you prefer, selecting a verse for each day on a particular topic, such as "principles," "promises," or "disciplines." After the notebook was put together, Bill let his kids use their creative art skills on the binder and pages so that it became a fun, family keepsake.

Devotions over dinner are the best time for their family. They try to keep them relatively short and to the point so that the kids are impacted by God's Word without losing focus. They also ask their kids questions about the verse to get them thinking about what it means and how to apply it to their lives, with the parents contributing simple examples from their own lives as well. Lastly, they take turns each evening ending the devotion time with prayer.

Many parents do not feel qualified to teach their children from the Bible. Nothing could be further from the truth! That's exactly what Satan wants you to believe. If you can read, you can teach. In fact, the best way to learn is through teaching. There are many resources and wise guides available to help you teach your children. And Bill reminds parents not to worry about missing a day here and there. The most important thing is working toward consistency.

Celebrate a rite of passage: The next idea came from the many Bar Mitzvahs and Bat Mitzvahs that the Gaultieres attend in their close-knit community, where many Jewish families live. They loved the idea of welcoming their own children into manhood or womanhood and preparing them for taking responsibility for their individual relationships with God, so they decided to develop a similar "rite of passage" for their own children.

With the help of a book called *Spiritual Milestones: a guide to celebrating your children's spiritual passages*, they decided that the rite of passage would include a developmental process for each child beginning at the age of fourteen, leading up to a ceremony. For this process, Bill and Kristi pick mentors for their children who can "disciple" them in different areas of their maturity over a two-year period.

"We wanted them to see and learn from others who loved the Lord and who were following and serving Him as well," Kristi says. "Sometimes familiarity breeds contempt—when we parents try to teach our children they're like, 'yeah we've heard this before.' But when they hear it from somebody else, it can really make a difference for them."

The Gaultieres encouraged their children to pick mentors in the following areas: relationship with God, relationships with the opposite sex and future marriage partner, career, spiritual friendships, ministry in the church, finances (including saving, tithing, and being a good steward), and their future family role. For their daughters, they added cooking and inner and outer beauty as a woman of God.

At age sixteen, after the mentoring process is complete, they hold the special rite of passage ceremony to which the mentors and their families are invited for a meaningful evening of pre-planned events. The schedule goes something like this:

- The child gives a message about what he/she learned from each of the mentors.
- Each mentor verbally affirms the child for something he or she particularly enjoyed or appreciated about their time together.

- The mentors get into a circle and invite the child into the center, symbolically welcoming him/her into manhood/womanhood.
- The child shares a slideshow of memorable times spent with each of the mentors.
- Bill presents the special, personalized Bible to the child at the end of the ceremony.
- The child is also presented with a scrapbook of letters written to him/her by each of the mentors before the ceremony, as well as pictures of their time together.
- A meal is shared to celebrate.

Their son, David, was the first to complete the program, and the Gaultieres have seen so much positive come out of it. "The biggest benefit has been in his confidence—it's made a *huge* difference," Kristi says. "The sense that he's grown into who God has made him to be, as well as his growth in interactions with others, has been immense. And the kids all love it, too. After watching big brother go through the process, our daughter Jenny couldn't wait for her turn to get started.

"I think that our goal is for them to really want to be apprentices of Jesus," Kristi says with enthusiasm. "We want them to follow Jesus, living their lives how He would want them to if He were with them, using their individual personalities, gifts, and talents. We want them to participate with Him in what He's doing now and what He wants to do through them."

Jack and Kim Anderson

Jack and Kim Anderson of Denver, Colorado, happen to be two more homeschooling parents who share some arrow strategies that have worked successfully for them:

Don't underestimate them: The Andersons have always tried to convey belief in the competence of their kids—for what they could learn and do—even at young ages. "We've always tried to give them as much as they could handle intellectually, and we've always given them the dignity of expecting them to contribute to the family in some way. Whether it was just picking up their own toys or helping with housework, or later on taking on things that were more intensive."[16]

Make it real: "We try to spend as little time as possible on 'busy work,'" says Kim. "In our school work, we don't read a lot of textbooks, we read a lot of primary sources." For instance, instead of reading *about* Shakespeare, or Milton, or Hemingway, the kids actually read their works. And instead of reading history textbooks, they read biographies and work on living history projects. Instead of just writing papers, they try to find a way to use them to make an impact by getting them published in a forum or using their information in a speech. The Andersons feel in this way, their kids are not just practicing for life, they're engaging in the real thing.

Challenge their motives: Whether it's onstage with performing arts, giving a speech or presentation, or whatever they are doing that involves others, the Andersons ask their kids, "How are you serving people through this?" This helps their kids to keep the focus off themselves, while training them to think about how their gifts in action can positively influence others.

Teach them to think "big picture": After noticing how much importance the Bible puts on genealogies and family tribes, Jack always encourages his kids to think about future generations and how their actions today might impact generations to come. "It's all based on family, and having the long-term vision that eventually our seeds will become like the sands of the ocean." Jack believes if our children will focus on leaving behind a spiritual legacy, it can be a type of "procreational evangelism."

"If they do things correctly, they can leave a positive mark for generations," Jack says. To this end, the Andersons challenge their kids to think in terms of blocks by asking them questions such as, "Where do you want to be in ten years?" And in terms of history, he encourages them to think about how they're fitting into the big picture of what God is doing, and what He's been up to in terms of 100 or even 500-year blocks.

Embracing this long-term thinking for her kids, Kim says, "When I was a teenager, my mom gave me a sort of legacy, or a vision. While praying about the future of her children, God gave her a verse, and it's been a guiding star for me as a parent. Isaiah 58:12 says, 'Your people will rebuild the ancient ruins and will raise up the age-old foundations; you will be called Repairer of Broken Walls, Restorer of Streets with Dwellings' (NIV). God is about healing things that are broken. And in raising my children, I'm always asking, *what are the 'ancient ruins' that need to be rebuilt? Where have the 'walls been broken,' and what are the 'streets that need to be restored'?*"

The Ferwerda Two Cents

As I've thought about these strategies for parenting with purpose, I've realized that most of them really are just lifestyle practices incorporated into daily training. I love the opportunity we've had to peek into the homes of wise guides to see what is working. While I could have done so much more if I'd had the information and expertise available, I did implement a few habits of my own with my kids that I believe made (or will make) a difference.

Dive deep into the Word: After a few years of reading through the *One Year Bible* on my own, I decided to start making notes for my kids of the many amazing things God has shown me in His Word through deeper study. My whole understanding of Scripture has been revolutionized by studying Jewish culture and tradition, history as it relates to the Bible and the Church, doing Internet research, and implementing a layman's study of Greek. Studying and compiling all my notes has been about a two-year process where I'm working toward giving them to my girls in a binder that they can use along with their daily Bible reading. My only regret is not having done this when they were younger.

To benefit other families, this Bible commentary will be posted in a blog format (downloadable) as a growth tool on our *OneMillionArrows. com* website. Moving through the daily Bible readings and commentary, you will learn history, symbolism, cultural implications, Messianic Jewish perspectives, prophecy interpretation, and how the Old Testament ties together with the New Testament perfectly in one cohesive message.

Turn everyday experiences into teaching moments: There's almost always a "story behind the story" in the course of daily life that can be used as a teaching tool of faith, especially from nature and human behavior. For instance, once our family majorly pruned a dead-looking tree that turned into an amazing, flourishing tree the next growing season. We used the lesson to teach our girls about the pruning process God uses in our lives to bring about spiritual health and beauty of character. Another time we used the profuse littering of discarded, plastic shopping bags around town, and even along the country highways, to teach them about Satan's lies that are so prevalent that they become unnoticed in our daily lives. This led to a great discussion of some of the specific lies he uses on each of us in everyday life. I have discovered that some of the most opportune times for connecting with my kids in this way—when they are the most receptive—are when we're in the car, at meal times, and at bedtime.

Keep a prayer journal: This can be a fantastic way to invest prayer tangibly in your kids' lives. Not only will you have a record of your prayers, but also someday when your kids are older, you can give it to them as a faith builder when they see God's answers to your prayers on their behalf. At that time they will also be touched by your intimate love and effort invested through the years just for them. These are freeform prayers. I pray anything—needs, spiritual warfare, Scripture verses, and anything else on my heart. I also write letters of love and blessing to my girls, knowing how special those words will become later. This can be a great (positive) release for writing to your kids when there are things you can't say now when they are too young to process it, but you want them to know, such as in the case of rebellion, divorce, illness, or times when the relationship is strained.

Engage in fasting prayers: An often-overlooked practice of the early church is fasting prayers. Whether implementing a regular day of fasting for your children (once a week) or keeping fasting prayers during times of special problems, challenges, or rebellion, this is a great and anointed way to battle in the unseen realms for the hearts of our children.

Let me encourage you in the case where you, by no choice of your own, have little influence in your kids' daily lives, such as in the case of divorce or after they leave home. Never underestimate the power of prayer. There was a point in my kids' upbringing after divorce when I worried about the results of their time away from my care and spiritual nurturing. "Lord," I prayed, "who will help my kids develop a passion for You and Your Word when I'm not with them?" The Lord put my fears to rest through the story of Joseph, one of the twelve sons of Jacob.

Joseph (Genesis 37–47) grew up to have a heart of integrity and deep love for the Lord and His purposes, despite many obstacles and difficulties in his early years. These obstacles included the death of his mother when he was a young child and being largely raised and influenced by strangers in a pagan country during his young adult life. But many years later we hear from Joseph's own lips, "I am a God-fearing man . . ." (Genesis 42:17–18). As an adult, Joseph also displays spiritual wisdom and understanding of the ways of God when he says to his brothers, "God has sent me here to keep you and your families alive so that you will become a great nation. Yes, it was God who sent me here, not you!" (Genesis 45:7–8).

Through this account, God reassured me that if I still do my part in praying for my children and teaching them to live by His Word when possible, He will still nurture and raise them up for His purposes during times when my influence is hindered. He's responsible for what takes place in their hearts and for the outcome of their lives. Just like Paul understood and stated in 1 Corinthians 3:6, "My job was to plant the seed in your hearts, and Apollos watered it, but it was God, not we, who made it grow." As I watch Him faithfully take care of the outcome, I can rest in Him.

My Part vs. God's Part

Whoa! That's a lot of stuff to take in. Do I have to do all of that, you ask? Maybe you're thinking you'll have to give up your day job just to have the time to train your children. These are all principles and creative strategies from others, but notice that each family does what they can do, and no two homes look alike. You can pick and choose from the buffet of ideas that resonate with your family's needs, personalities, and abilities, or you can come up with your own ideas. The sky is the limit for creatively investing in your children, but the goal is the same: *get the Word into your kids*—into their minds, their hearts, and their character.

Have you noticed the other, indispensable common denominator among arrow-raising parents? They aren't content to sit by, watching their kids figure out the answers by themselves. They don't do passive parenting. They show the way by example, and then they expect *a lot* from their kids. Expecting a lot won't kill anyone, but it does require crucial follow through and focused, active parenting using our secret formula: training = teaching + modeling + accountability. It also requires belief in your kids—that they are capable and gifted human beings with a lot to offer the world *today* . . . not in ten or twenty years.

And don't miss this important factor. Every single one of our featured parents' grown children is committed to changing his or her world for Christ. How do those kinds of odds happen unless these parents know and live a successful process that many other parents don't?

I believe that when parents have the *mindset* of making arrows instead of just raising good and happy kids, the results speak for themselves. When we take to heart that *the home*—not the church, not the youth programs, not the Christian school—is the Great Commission Training Center, the lives of our kids are truly impacted soul deep. I'm not saying for a second that this can only be accomplished by homeschooling—my own kids are not homeschooled. I'm saying that we can't leave the real spiritual training of our kids up to anybody else. This is our baby—literally—and we have to take the training years seriously.

No longer can our lives and schedules *revolve around* sports, entertainment, amusement, busyness, or a host of other "good" or even "good enough" activities. They must revolve around *best*, through getting to know God very personally, glorifying and enjoying Him, and then bringing His Good News to others. Sure we can still be involved in those things, but they cannot be allowed to dictate our schedules to the point that there is no time for spiritual training and involvement in *the mission*.

What exactly is *my part* of arrow-parenting, and what is *God's part*, we ask? So much of it is out of my control, yet undoubtedly I still have great responsibility in it, too. I believe the answer is found in 1 Chronicles 28:20. The Lord's Temple is under construction, and David exhorts his workers: "Be strong and courageous, and do the work. Don't be afraid or discouraged by the size of the task, for the LORD God, my God, is with you. He will not fail you or forsake you. He will see to it that all the work related to the Temple of the LORD is finished correctly."

As we raise our kids in the instruction of the Lord, we must realize that they are little "temples of God" under construction (see 1 Corinthians 6:19). That means we parents are in partnership with God as temple builders. According to this verse, my part as a temple-builder is *the work*— barring all shortcuts. Not hiring out the work to someone else. As I have contemplated what this means, practically speaking, I think my part as a parent is teaching my children through instruction and modeling to learn and live by God's Word in everyday life (Deuteronomy 11:18–19), teaching them how to enjoy Him through an intimate relationship (Isaiah 43:10), consistently disciplining them in love (Hebrews 12:5–11), and persistently praying for them (Ephesians 1:16–20).

In doing this, I must be careful. I can teach them these things without fail, but if I'm not modeling them in my own life, my kids will see only hypocrisy. My best efforts will mean nothing. True temple building must be approached as an all encompassing project, a serious 24/7 undertaking. Temple building is never complete until our children are able to stand on their own as strong and sturdy structures, taking hold of *the mission* for themselves.

Thankfully, as we parents forge out into the unknown complexities of temple building, we are never alone. God holds the blueprints for our children's lives, and His role is the overseer and general contractor of the outcome, giving us what we need as we actively seek to do the work. We do the work; He does *the rest*. He sees it through to completion, and where there is devoted, serious temple building going on, He will not fail us.

Now that we've discovered how to perpetuate *the mission* at home, it's time to look at the second essential vehicle. Have you ever considered raising more kids?

CHAPTER 6

SHAPE ARROWS
BEYOND

Remember this—a farmer who plants only a few seeds will get a small crop. But the one who plants generously will get a generous crop.

—2 Corinthians 9:6

God is pursuing with omnipotent passion a worldwide purpose of gathering joyful worshipers for Himself from every tribe and tongue and people and nation . . . Therefore, let us bring our affections into line with His, and, for the sake of His name, let us renounce the quest for worldly comforts and join His global purpose.

—John Piper[1]

Edward Lorenz, a mathematician and meteorologist at MIT, discovered through experiments with mathematical equations in 1961 that the flap of a single butterfly's wings in South America could actually start a chain of events that impacted the weather all the way up in North America. And according to his findings, one flap of a seagull's wings could forever alter weather patterns.[2]

If a single butterfly can leave a mark on the world through simply doing what it was made to do—flapping its wings—what could we accomplish as humans made in God's image if we were to do what God has made us to do? As parents using our gifts and abilities for *the mission*, what could we accomplish by investing in one more child (or even a few) in order to effect change that carries into other countries and even continents? What would it look like?

Imagine for a moment that, like Papa, you decide to add to your quiver one abandoned child who needs a second chance at a purposeful life. So you adopt a baby boy from Africa. Say your efforts successfully sharpen this uniquely gifted young man as a faithful and empowered arrow of God who devotes himself wholeheartedly to *the mission*. As he grows up, he decides to go back to his native country as a missionary. Sharing the Gospel wherever he goes, he leads many to Christ, and those new believers begin sharing Christ, too. Pretty soon, whole families become believers and they begin spreading the Good News within their communities. After a lifetime, the web of lives you've impacted for eternity by that decision to parent one more child in addition to your own is more than you could possibly have imagined.

But then, go a step further. Imagine after you die and are resurrected into your real home, God puts on a little party in your honor. To this "little get together," He invites all the people whose lives have been rescued and impacted spiritually as a result of your intentional decision to invest in a child outside your own biological family. There are so many people in attendance that you can't even count them all—happy, smiling people, from villages and even cities all over Africa, hugging, laughing, and expressing their gratitude to you for giving them a chance to hear the Good News about Jesus. What amazing eternal returns on your relatively small investment of flapping your wings just to parent one more child.

Guess what? *You can do this.* Starting right now, you can adopt an orphan quite literally, or you can also ripple this kind of butterfly effect throughout the world without even going to the effort of actually raising any more kids in your home. The hard work of gathering and raising these children is already being done for you, if you so choose. Thanks to the many arrow ministries already in operation worldwide, including the U.S., you can easily invest in arrow shaping without changing your family dynamics or routine!

Shaping arrows beyond means that we are looking outside our own families for ways to invest in *the mission* through the lives of others. After all, every person and every family shoulders the responsibility of the Great Commission—to go and make disciples of all nations (Matthew 28:18–20). No exceptions. So why not invest in tomorrow's generation—the kids who could change the course of a country and go down in His-Story?

As Americans, you and I, without a doubt, have the financial resources, with a little priority rearranging, to "go to nations" with our efforts or at least our money, by investing in young people who are being shaped by many different arrow ministries. While adoption of these kids is a great option for some families, I'm also excited about investing in kids who are currently being raised up in their own cultures to bring lasting change through the love of Christ to their local villages, cities, and countries. As we take this step, we teach our children the second part of the two fold, crucial component of arrow making (after becoming an arrow) of investing in other arrows that are carrying the love of God where we are not able to go. And I think investing in other *kids* is one of the best ways to get our kids spiritually and emotionally engaged in this aspect of *the mission.*

There are many great arrow-shaping ministries for children, both nationally and internationally, and we'll discuss in coming chapters some of the ways to get involved. For work in other countries, I recommend investing in organizations that are shaping children through the means of special orphanages or homes—24/7 environments—designed specifically to develop children for *the mission* and to nurture them in all areas of life. Some of the great arrow-type ministries following this kind of discipleship model on several continents, including Papa's, are listed in the resources section at the end of the book. Two ministries in particular that are networking every aspect of orphan care worldwide are the Christian Alliance for Orphans, and Viva Network (Patrick McDonald of chapter 4).

Closer to home, there are also many opportunities to invest in American kids doing short-term missions to other countries, (investing in your own kids' missions experiences is the first priority, of course). This worthy investment helps interested young people develop a heart for *the mission* and gives them a chance to learn about other cultures. Many kids come from families that can't afford to send their kids on mission trips, but they still have the desire to make a difference and to use their God-given talents on the mission field.

One youth ministry that's drawing teens from all over the country for various aspects of ministry, Teen Mania, has a heartbeat "to provoke a young generation to passionately pursue Jesus Christ and to take His life-giving message to the ends of the earth." A non-denominational ministry, they provide evangelism and service opportunities for preteens, teens, and young adult leaders on six continents for short-term trips. To date, they have taken over 50,000 teen missionaries to fifty countries around the globe.[3] My older daughter has been to both Brazil and Peru with this ministry and had fantastic, life-changing experiences on both trips.

Youth with a Mission (YWAM) also began as a non-denominational youth missionary ministry, but now includes all ages. They have operations in 160 countries and have over 16,000 full-time volunteer workers in 1,100 locations internationally. They train 25,000 short-term missionaries annually.[4]

What a great investment, keeping our young people engaged in *the mission* by helping them reach out to the world!

A very cool spin on investing in children outside your own home and even outside your country is this: *You don't have to biologically reproduce in order to become a spiritual parent.* Spiritual parenting can be just as meaning-ful and impacting as traditional parenting in matters of eternity, and can take on many forms. You can invest time, talents, prayer, money, possessions, and skills into shaping kids locally, nationally, or even internationally.

Papa had his own biological children, but God showed him through-out the years that spiritual parenting—whether his own kids or others who have no spiritual guidance or heritage—is one of the most important investments of his time on this earth. Whether it be Papa launching thousands of sharpened arrows each year and unleashing the Gospel into the lives of many thousands more, or you and me investing in as many children as possible in whatever ways we can, our spiritual offspring could potentially be limitless.

Now that could turn into some party!

Kids on a Mission

There's nothing quite so amazing as being awakened at the crack of dawn to the sound of little kids worshiping God in song at the tops of their lungs. Who in the world could stay in bed and miss out on that? In my recent trips overseas, I've had this magical experience in both cities and remote, tribal villages. It's my favorite part of the trips.

In such places, I've met children who are being shaped into arrows by loving and devoted workers. These children have everything they need because of financial supporters, mainly in America, who are faithfully in-vesting in them financially and prayerfully. For kids who live in these true arrow homes, every day of their lives is a training day. Just like any good family, there is love, discipline, and plenty of responsibility. And the kids carry that sense of family into their adult lives, feeling the continuing love and support of their adoptive homes. Both the workers who are physically raising them on the field and the financial supporters who are making it possible are engaged in a team effort of spiritually parenting these kids. Without either part of the team, there would be no way to ready these kids for *the mission*.

I believe these previously unwanted kids have been chosen by God to reap a great harvest of souls in their countries by using their unique backgrounds, gifts, and passion for the Gospel. Who's to say the child I invest in can't become the next Papa in his (or her) own country, or the next Billy Graham or Ron Luce (Teen Mania) in ours? I believe God is going to specifically credit and reward those who invest in any way in His kids who have been set apart for *the mission*. Just think, your family could invest in a young woman like Jennie.

Jennie

Jennie knows nothing about her south India parents except that, as a newborn, they threw her away and left her for dead in a city dumpster. Some college boys happened by and heard her crying, so they picked her up out of the garbage and took her to a nearby orphanage.

Jennie was so bright that she graduated from Bible college at sixteen. Her instructors noticed how mature and responsible she was at such a young age and how she had a heart for helping children, so they sent her to help out at an orphanage for younger children for one year of on-the-job training. When the main caregiver at that orphanage was called to another location to help out during a time of need, seventeen-year-old Jennie took over. For the past two years, she's been taking care of an entire orphanage of eight younger children with the help of an assistant, Mary, who's now sixteen and also an orphan.

This position is a good fit for Jennie, who loves kids and feels privileged to serve them. "You don't have to give up everything you love to make a difference," she says. "It starts by thinking about others, then showing them the love that God has shown you. In this way He will use you to transform lives."[5]

God is definitely using Jennie's love, experiences, and training to do just that for the little ones under her care. "When the children get sad and start crying for their parents, I can understand their pain and comfort them better than anyone else because I've been in their shoes. I'm able to give the love and care that they want and need, just like my caretakers showed me God's love when I was a child. I feel like a mother to them now."

Understandably, Jennie gets tired and discouraged with so much responsibility on her young shoulders. Some of the kids are mischievous, and sometimes food for the kids is in short supply during periods of financial hardship or persecution on the ministry. At those times, she wonders if she's doing the right thing. But then she remembers that when she came to work at the orphanage, she committed herself to serving the orphans with her best efforts. So instead of fretting, Jennie says she prays, asking God to give her strength to continue taking care of them. She relies on Him to be her protector and provider, her Father and Mother—her everything.

Her faith has grown immensely as a result of relying on God's provision and care. Once, when her cupboards were bare, God miraculously supplied food from neighbors. Another time, when one of the children missed the school bus, a man stopped by unexpectedly to see if she needed anything, so he was able to take the girl to school.

Once an orphan, now taking care of orphans, does Jennie have any regrets? "If I didn't know Jesus, I wouldn't be serving these children now. I'd be out living on the streets—if I was even alive." She believes that she will raise these kids to grow up and take care of others in the same way.

Imagine that. Young Jennie—an arrow raising more arrows. It's exciting to think how far reaching your influence could be on a young life like Jennie's by spiritually parenting her through financial support.

Lily

A thousand miles away, in a remote tribal village of northeastern India, Lily is another young woman making a mark on the world. When she was thirteen, children in her village began showing up at her house during her visits home on school breaks, asking her to teach them. Boarding at an orphanage in a village some distance away from her home, just so she could attend school, Lily became the most educated person in her whole village, one of the few who could read. It was her dream to someday return to her village and open a school.

Now Lily is twenty-one, and her dream is becoming a reality. With high school and Bible college under her belt, she has moved back to her family's village, where fifty-seven kids come to her every day for schooling. The village families are so excited about this; they have begun looking for some land where they can build a school for her to teach their children.

"The parents of the children believe in me and trust me to teach their children," says Lily. "They have been so encouraging." Sadly, this contrasts the opinions of her family and friends, who think Lily is too quiet and fragile to run a school by herself. "They don't know who I am on the inside," Lily confides. "I may seem unable, small, and weak on the outside, but I'm a very strong person on the inside."[6]

Lily is most excited about how she will impact her village with the love of Christ. The first subject she teaches every day is biblical studies, and after school she offers a devotional time with singing and more Bible teaching. She says her students are enthusiastic in learning about God and the Bible. Eventually she hopes to start more schools in other, nearby villages.

There are many Lilys who need faithful partners in order to bring Christ back to their own people. How amazing would it be for your family to know you were helping teach fifty-seven kids in a remote village you'd never even seen? The party is still growing.

Justin

Closer to home, maybe you could also add a young man like Justin Dobrenz to your growing spiritual family. I first met Justin when he was working at a Christian summer youth camp in northern Wyoming. Anyone who chooses to take care of manic, mischievous kids 24/7 for an entire summer has to either be in the witness protection program, or quite possibly have a total heart for kid ministry. But rumor has it that the perks are more than worth it—"refreshing" early morning showers, completely restful sleep between three and six a.m., and just enough summer earnings to cover your travel expenses back to college. For me, it sounds about as much fun as the dental school root canal volunteer program, or maybe a third world boot camp in Phoenix in July. But for Justin, and many of the other awesome counselors who come back year after year to serve and mentor kids, it is being an arrow.

After two years as a camp counselor, Justin decided to do something a little less dangerous (and more relaxing) than entertaining today's youth. He decided to become a Bible smuggler. At age twenty-one he went to work for Vision Beyond Borders, an organization that specializes in taking translated Bibles and evangelistic tools into the underground church in China and other parts of Asia, as well as Cuba, Turkey, Morocco, and Romania, with the purpose of equipping the local people for *the mission*. Currently this organization has hand-delivered over 600,000 contraband Bibles worldwide.

Every three months or so, several times a day, Justin tirelessly smuggled a backbreaking load of Bibles across borders on foot. He's had many opportunities to make a difference in the lives of believers who are hungry for the Word, as well as to see God miraculously open the way for him to get across borders under the noses of intimidating and suspicious border guards.

Without a doubt, Justin is an arrow. And while he has loving parents who are very supportive of his call to *the mission*, he's like the many other young arrows in our own country who could always benefit from having more adoptive spiritual parents who are willing to invest prayerfully and financially in his world-changing ministry endeavors. He has ongoing travel expenses, not to mention the ministry can always use more Bibles and teaching materials. In fact, when you invest in someone like Justin, you're taking the Word of God either into places it has never been or places it's not allowed, becoming a spiritual parent to many in the underground, persecuted church. Can you imagine the radiant joy on all those faces at your party?

Shannon

Being an arrow doesn't come easily for Shannon Patrick. She grew up in a broken home with a single mom, and it wasn't until her first year at college that she got serious about her faith. At that time, she went on an overseas mission trip with an international youth missions organization (unnamed for security reasons), and some of the leaders told her that, as part of their discipleship program, they wanted her to consider becoming a trainer of other youth missionaries. "I folded my arms and said, 'I'll *never* do that,'" Shannon remembers.

A while later, back at college, she was brushing her teeth one night when God clearly said, "You're going to be a missionary trainer."

"No, I won't do it! That's too scary," Shannon argued. But a few months later, God won, and Shannon attended a seven-month program in Germany. Part of her training included going into a Muslim country for two months to "teach English." This was a great experience for Shannon, but still she wrestled constantly with feelings of fear and inadequacy.

"For some of the kids it's no big deal to do this kind of work. But for me, it's a *big deal* because I feel totally under-qualified." By being faithful to His call, Shannon discovered that during these stretching times, God becomes her adequacy. Once when she had to find a creative and covert way to present the Gospel story to Muslim children, she asked God to help her. That day He gave her an awesome version of the Gospel story about a Prince and a King that the kids were totally into. "When I began to narrate, suddenly God's peace came into the room and settled on the kids. You could feel it. It was really neat."

After her seven months in training, Shannon is now ready for training missionaries, which will include leading her own outreaches to foreign countries. But at times she still struggles with trusting God with the unknown of her future. "It's really frightening. Even though God knows what's best for me, and my life is not my own anymore, *I'm scared.* There are a lot of challenges that I'll have to face. I think I know in my heart what God's character is like, but I still struggle with questions like, *Lord, what are You going to make me go through?*"[7]

Some of Shannon's family members think she should forget about missions for now and focus on finishing college. With the fear bearing down on her, Shannon is often tempted to agree. "I worry about the practical things like, *what am I going to do about money?*"

For now, Shannon has decided to put off college to pursue *the mission*, training young missionaries to span the globe. "I'm working on living in the present moment and trusting God with the rest, but there's still that fear. It takes practice to overcome. It would be so much easier for me to go to college and start pursuing a normal life where I could start earning money and be comfortable. But I really can't do anything else. I don't want to miss out on what God has for me."

Imagine how many lives you could reach by investing in an arrow like Shannon, who is equipping young people to go to countries worldwide to spread the Gospel.

Just like all these arrows beyond, as long as your kids live in your home, every day of their lives can and should be a mission-training day. Every Christian home in America is a potential Bible college.

Is the investment worth it? Let the kids' lives speak for themselves. When you invest in mission experiences for your own kids, you give them a heart etched with concern for *the mission*. When you invest in a person like Jennie, you also invest in the eight kids she's raising to continue the process of hope. When you invest in someone like Lily, you also invest in the fifty-seven plus kids who will carry the Good News back to their families and villages. When you invest in someone like Justin, you're taking the Word of God into places it's desperately needed, bringing light and hope to many in the underground, persecuted church. When you invest in someone like Shannon, you're helping train missionaries to reach over a hundred different countries.

Maybe you've never thought about investing in kids outside your own home. But think of it this way. Investing in mission-minded young people means becoming a spiritual parent, leaving a world-changing legacy for those you've never even met. And it's never too late to get started making a huge difference. You and your family can personally play a role in impacting lives in villages, cities, and even countries, whether or not any of you ever set foot there. Now that is truly multiplication at its best.

Let the party begin!

CHAPTER 7

MOBILIZE BOWS

Sodom's sins were pride, laziness, and gluttony, while the poor and needy suffered outside her door.

—Ezekiel 16:49

Only during the few years of this life are we given the privilege of serving each other and Christ. We shall have heaven forever, but only a short time for service here, and therefore we must not waste the opportunity.

—Sadhu Sundar Singh

There was a certain rich man going on a lengthy business trip. Being a compassionate sort, he called together his estate caretakers and gave them each some money to invest in helping the poor while he was gone, namely orphaned kids, who were near and dear to his heart.

To his personal bookkeeper, he gave the means to financially help ten children. To his housekeeper, he gave the means to help five children. And to his gardener, who was not known for managing money well, which is why he wasn't a bookkeeper, he still gave plenty to help take care of at least one needy child.

When he returned home a long while later, he asked the bookkeeper what happened. "Well, you gave me enough to help ten children. I invested part of the money in a mutual fund and earned so much, I had enough left over after helping ten children to buy myself a really nice, new, high-speed water-ski boat. But I just didn't feel right using the money on myself like that. I mean, what good is a ski boat when others aren't even able to eat? So I used the money to help ten more kids get rescued from a poverty-stricken life, providing plenty of money to raise them in Christ-centered homes."

"Well done! I am so proud of you, because you did exactly what I would have done with my money. You were a faithful money manager, so now I know I can trust you. I will give you even more ways you can help save poor and needy children, because of my great love for them. They're going to change the world, you know. Just for this, I guarantee you will get a huge year-end bonus! Please, I insist you take a nice, paid vacation for all your hard work and faithfulness."

Next he turned to the housekeeper. "So what happened to the money I gave you?"

"Sir, you gave me enough to help five children, which I did right away. I also got a part-time job while you were gone for some extra spending money. I worked long enough to save the money to buy a plasma flat screen TV that I've been eyeing down at CHEAPCO. But when I thought about the money you had given me for the children, and how so many more were still out there, I just couldn't bring myself to spend the money on myself so greedily, so I was able to help an additional five children get plenty of food and medical treatment, not to mention excellent Bible training!"

"Wow, that's amazing! I am so proud of you, because you did exactly what I would have done. Not only did you use my money wisely, but you also sacrificed your own time and energy to make a difference. You were a faithful money manager, so now I know I can trust you. I will give you even more ways you can help the poor. You too will get a nice, fat bonus this year. Get ready; you'll have a hard time spending it all! Now, please, take your family on a relaxing vacation, my treat."

Finally the estate owner turned to his gardener. "So what happened with the money I gave you? I'll bet you really did something great with it, too, huh?"

"Well, uh, sort of. I know you have high standards and hate careless spending. You expect a lot from us, for sure. When I saw how many orphans needed help, I was overwhelmed. I'm only one person, after all. How could I make a difference, especially with how little money you gave me to spend? And even if I did give it to help a child, how could I be sure the child actually received it? I was worried about your money being mishandled and unaccounted for. Also, I was afraid I might disappoint you with how little I was able to do, especially compared to what the others were doing. I'm not that good with money—you know that already. Anyhow, I dug a hole in the back yard and kept your money nice and safe. Here it is, not a penny missing."

The estate owner was furious. "That's a terrible way to live! It's criminal to live so cautiously! If you knew I was expecting only the best from you, why did you choose to do less than nothing? The least you could have done would have been to give the money to a homeless shelter or a struggling single mother. You're fired! And I'll see to it you never get a job in this part of the country again."

"To those who use well what they are given, even more will be given, and they will have an abundance. But from those who are unfaithful, even what little they have will be taken away" (Matthew 25:29).

Faithful Servants?

Right now, in countries all over the world, through dozens of ministries, there are many thousands of children being gathered from hopeless, purposeless lives and being shaped into arrows. These ministries have plenty of broken branches to gather, and they've got the archers, who are the workers, in place to train and send the fully formed arrows.

But what about the bows?

The bows are the resources—especially the financial investments—that make it possible for this process to work. Without bows, arrows are completely useless. Without the financial means to be shaped and launched, there is little point in gathering. For too long, many of the bows have been broken, disabled, or hidden away.

What's the big deal if your family invests in other arrows in other parts of the world or not? Look around you. God has entrusted Americans, especially many Christians, with more wealth and resources than people in any other country. Not sure where I got this notion? I don't know . . . perhaps from the certain types of cars filling the parking lots of certain types of church buildings . . . . But I do know one thing: more money funneling into our eager little hands does not mean *more blessed*; it means *more responsibility*.

God did not provide abundantly for us so that we can use our resources selfishly. He did it so that we would be His money managers, using what He's given us faithfully for *the mission* of temple building and arrow production worldwide. Contributing to the work in other lives and countries is a crucial characteristic of being an arrow. Why? Because, given the opportunity, these young people in other countries will be able to reach places we could never reach alone. Without them, we cannot fulfill *the mission*. They can't do it without us; we can't do it without them.

Before I had my first real-life glimpse at the work being done on behalf of destitute children in other countries, and back when starving, homeless people probably remained unnoticed on my way out of the grocery store with my cart billowing over with food, I had four major mental obstacles to investing in *the mission* and suffering of others.

⇥   There are too many needs—I can't make a difference.

↦ The mission field is not for everyone.

↦ I don't know if my money is being used for the intended purpose.

↦ But wait, what about "The American Dream"?

Too many needs: Short of watching a Miss America Pageant, there was no ready answer I knew of for solving world hunger. The magnitude of the need was most discouraging when I began considering my part in alleviating suffering. I wondered what in the world my little $30 a month, or any other seemingly insignificant donations to relief funds and charities, was going to do, really. In the grand scheme, I figured *nothing*. The person I feed today will just get hungry again tomorrow. One meal—or even a few—isn't going to change the course of a life. Besides, as soon as I feed one, there are a thousand lined up right behind. This is what I thought.

Then I had a sudden opportunity to go to Haiti, in November of 2006, which began the series of strange, life-changing events that soon led me to meet Papa in India. In Haiti, I met Willio, a man whose compassionate generosity belied the desperation of his environment—an environment that turns many innocent victims into hardened criminals bent on survival. The despair in Haiti is beyond comprehension, and it's certainly apparent in the widespread lawlessness and corruption.

Growing up with his grandparents in Haiti, the poorest country in the western hemisphere, Willio suffered intensely from hunger and, at times, even thirst. This made concentrating in school practically impossible, and frequently he'd get lost in daydreams about food. The few times he ventured over to his dad's house to see if he might get some paper or pencils for school or maybe a bite to eat, his deadbeat dad, who sired 38 kids yet fathered none, chased him away, bellowing, "Go away! Don't ever come back here again!"

When thirsty, Willio often scooped stagnant water out of holes where rain had collected in the ground. In Willio's world, dysentery, malaria, yellow fever, tuberculosis, and AIDS are a part of everyday living—and dying.

A couple years back, Willio began taking in children off the street to protect them and to feed them when possible, which was only about one meal every three days. Finally, fearing starvation for his household, he went down to an "Internet Café" in his hometown, consisting of a couple of old computers hooked up to a generator, and typed the word "hope" into an Internet search engine. When this brought up an American-based ministry, Willio sent a desperate S.O.S., asking for food and assistance.

God did indeed send hope to Willio and his household through the ministry, and it soon became possible for him to begin taking in even more children off the streets. He now raises these kids with a heart to become spiritual leaders of Haiti. Willio believes it's time for a change in Haiti, but he believes it must start with the children. With that in mind, he also opened a day school for poverty-stricken kids who have no other learning options. The enrollment is currently nearing 1,000 kids, and the school is a medium for kids to get in on daily Bible teaching and spiritual guidance. In his "spare time," he pastors a fast-growing church, attended mostly by parents of the kids enrolled in his free school.

After meeting Willio and his kids, that "insignificant," monthly donation suddenly turned into new life for one hopeless, living, breathing child with a name and a face. It turned into the potential of raising a future world-changer with an education and the love of God. If that one hopeless child were my child, would that monthly amount seem a little more significant?

After I returned from Haiti, I tried to put this concept into words. How could I explain to people that giving for even one child really could make a difference? Then I found the perfect words—the starfish story, by Loren Eiseley. Here's the shortened, paraphrased version:

> One day a man walked along the shore after a storm, and as
> he looked down the beach, he noticed a younger man, reach-
> ing down to the shore, picking up small objects, and throwing

them into the ocean. As he came close to the younger man, he inquired, "What are you doing?"

The young man replied, "Throwing starfish back into the ocean—before they die."

The older gentleman said, "But, young man, do you not realize that there are miles and miles of beach and there are starfish all along every mile? You can't possibly make a difference!"

At this, the young man bent down, picked up yet another starfish, and threw it into the ocean. As it met the water he responded, "It made a difference for that one."[1]

I, too, want to make a difference, but I don't want to just feed stomachs. When I invest in suffering, I want to make sure I'm investing in hearts and souls as well. That's where true eternal change comes about, and that's what *the mission* is all about.

"I can't afford to give—I'm already stretched to the max," I used to console my conscience. Then I read how Jesus said that the measure of a person's heart can be gauged by where his money is going (Matthew 6:21). If I'm honest with myself, I'll admit it's my *priorities*, not my *bank account*—no matter how puny—that keeps me from giving extravagantly to God's work. I've watched myself on this. I'll spend money on hobbies, clothes, vacations, recreation, beauty treatments, enough books to start my own library, silly things not even on my shopping list, infomercial products that are going to change my life forever—you know, all the necessities— and then say that I don't have enough money for the offering plate or the missions fund on Sunday.

"As surely as the compass needle follows north," says Randy Alcorn in his book, *The Treasure Principle*, "your heart will follow your treasure. Money leads; hearts follow. I've heard people say, 'I want more of a heart for missions.' I always respond, 'Jesus tells you exactly how to get it. Put your money in missions—and in your church and the poor—and your heart will follow.'"[2]

Papa's son, Sam, told me some inspiring (and convicting) stories of people who have given money to the orphan ministry in recent years. One elderly woman lived on a small fixed income of Social Security. For fifteen years, she sent a dollar—one dollar—every month. Another couple in a similar situation mowed two lawns on weekends for more than twenty years to support one orphan.

One of Sam's recent favorites took place in a poor village in India on a Sunday evening. He'd spent all day traveling to over a dozen village churches to encourage them. It was well after dark, and he was exhausted after his last meeting, when an elderly village woman approached him with her grandson, asking Sam to pray for the boy. After he prayed, the woman took his hand and placed seven rupees (about fifteen cents) in it. "This is all I have to give to you. Thank you for praying for my grandson."

The local pastor told Sam that the woman didn't even have enough to feed her family and truly gave all she had. So moved with compassion by this woman's faith and generosity, Sam left her with seven hundred rupees to feed her family. "That was a defining moment in my life, a great moment in all my years of ministry, that this lady would give so much." Sam said it reminded him of a story of long ago.

"While Jesus was in the Temple, he watched the rich people putting their gifts into the collection box. Then a poor widow came by and dropped in two pennies. 'I assure you,' he said, 'this poor widow has given more than all the rest of them. For they have given a tiny part of their surplus, but she, poor as she is, has given everything she has'" (Luke 21:1–4).

But can my meager offering really make a difference, we ask?

"Jesus soon saw a great crowd of people climbing the hill, looking for him. Turning to Philip, he asked, 'Philip, where can we buy bread to feed all these people?' He was testing Philip, for he already knew what he was going to do.

"Philip replied, 'It would take a small fortune to feed them!'

"Then Andrew, Simon Peter's brother, spoke up. 'There's a young boy here with five barley loaves and two fish. But what good is that with this huge crowd?'" (John 6:5–9).

Don't miss this. A little kid shows up on the crowded hillside with only a sack lunch. Jesus, miracle worker and omnipotent provider, asks Philip where they're going to find enough food for over ten thousand people. Andrew pipes in, mentioning the boy's lunch, which seems ludicrous. But this story is about much more than a bunch of hungry people. It's about more than the financial fortune it would take to feed them all. This story is about what happens when God does the math.

The boy offered Jesus all he had. Jesus took it, small as it was, divided it, multiplied it, added up enough to fill everyone present, and then subtracted the remainder, which was way more than He started with—twelve baskets full of food. Now that's *Jesus Math*! Realize that, as He fed stomachs, He also fed a deeper hunger. Along with serving barley loaves, He served the Bread of Life.

We may feel that the amount we have to offer the physically hungry world is miniscule. We may feel that the amount we have to offer our own spiritually hungry kids is not enough. We may show up with our little brown bag, feeling tired, stressed, pulled from all sides, inadequate for the job, already aware that we are not doing all that we could or should be doing. But still, we're trying to do our best. We're offering what we do have. And that's where *Jesus Math* comes in. When we give Him what we do have, small as it is, we allow Him the opportunity to do the math for us. He takes the little we offer, asking for all we have to give upfront—our kids, our energy, our time, our money, our resources, our life—and then He makes a great, miraculous impact with it. And He gives much more back than we ever started with.

Papa says, "One of our greatest hindrances as parents is that we look to ourselves and ask, 'What can I do? What difference can I make? This task is impossible.' We forget that we are called on to do the impossible with the help of the God of possibilities. By using whatever we have, we're able to accomplish great things because God will multiply our efforts and resources.

"When I came to the Lord and gave Him my life, I did not have any bread or fish in my hand," says Papa. "But I began to distribute whatever He entrusted me with. Since then, I have received many baskets full of blessings in return. Instead of focusing on what you don't have or can't do, put all you do have into the hands of Jesus. Bring what you have to the Lord and trust Him to multiply it. Give thanks to God for the small things and use them for His Kingdom."

Not for everyone: *The Great Commission is only for missionary-types. I've met those people, and they're an odd bunch. C'mon, you'd have to have lost your mind to go hang out with headhunters in a jungle (think about it). No sir, not for me. I rather like my head attached, thank you very much.*

As we've already discussed at length, *the mission is* for everyone! And before we clutch at our necks with fear, remember what we learned in the last chapter. You can go without your body. Yep, you can be on the mission field, even in the Amazon, without losing your mind—uh, your head, that is.

You can go with your money.

You can go with your talents.

You can go with your prayers.

You can go with your children.

Even if you can't go in person, your money and your talents are a great substitute. There are amazingly creative and talented people all over this world, volunteering on their own or through programs (or even working vocationally) to build up missionaries with their willingness and abilities—designing websites; writing stories and testimonies for church newsletters, websites, books, and magazines; working directly for international ministries from the States; knitting hats; gathering blankets, clothes, and shoes; sending personal hygiene care packages; training in language or cultural skills; doing short-term missions trips for service or construction projects; and donating money from garage sales, bake sales, and other creative fundraisers. There are always many needs and just as many different ways to "go."

If you and your family aren't already doing anything world-impacting outside your home and community, sending your money is an excellent place to start. As you give, you begin to develop a love for and an interest in the people to whom you are giving. It breeds an increasing desire to get involved.

To obey Jesus' commands of sharing the Good News and helping the orphan, the widow, and those in need, you have to deliberately find a way to go. "Pure and lasting religion in the sight of God our Father means that we must care for orphans and widows in their troubles" (James 1:27). I believe the reason God called it "pure and lasting" is because it's the ultimate in selfless giving. These kinds of people could never repay us. When we give to them, we are not expecting anything in return, and we are never more like Jesus than when we give that selflessly.

If you can't go with your body, go some other way. Yes, *the mission* is for you.

Misused money: It seems we hear all too often about money being mishandled. Even in ministries, there are many hands exchanging funding before it ever reaches its final destination. How can we know for sure that our money is going to the cause or person for which we sent it? Wouldn't it be better to keep it than to find out later that it got wasted, squandered, or misused? Wouldn't that be irresponsible giving?

There's a balance here. We have to do our homework up front before we give to any organization. Research for yourself how donations are distributed and accounted for, and if it's positively or negatively affecting the native community. Ask the ministry what percentage of your donation is used for administrative costs (a good goal is 20 percent or less). Find out if they allow you to visit the field for yourself to see how your money is being used. Beyond that, we are called to give. We can't always police how it's used. How do we know when we put money in the offering plate on Sunday that it's not being misused or over-administrated somehow? How can we be sure that the money we give anywhere is being used correctly? The answer is, we can't. Not 100 percent of the time. Is that any reason to throw up our hands and forget about it?

Here's the truth that can give us a dose of peace about giving: *Giving is more for us than for the cause.* God isn't pining away, helpless to do something without our money. He already owns all the cattle on a thousand hills—and all the money, too. Where it's needed, God is ultimately the Provider. He cares more about the heart that gives the money than about where it's going or how it's used. The motivation to give should be about being obedient to His command to give sacrificially, to willingly do our part to fulfill *the mission*, and to develop a heart of compassion for others. Our loyalty is to Jesus first, the cause second. The outcome of our giving is ultimately His responsibility.

While we can do our best to invest responsibly, we can't totally micromanage it or we would drive everyone crazy. Besides, if our giving depended on 100 percent effective use by totally honest people, we could never give. That's not a bankable reality anywhere in this broken world. We must look at the big picture. Look for the fruit of the ministry and then conclude whether they are handling the money wisely by the lives that are being changed.

In 1 Chronicles 29:16–17, David is offering a prayer of thanksgiving after watching all the people donate generously from their hearts and possessions to the construction of the Temple. "O Lord our God, even these materials that we have gathered to build a Temple to honor your holy name come from you! It all belongs to you! I know, my God, that you examine our hearts and rejoice when you find integrity there. *You know I have done all this with good motives*, and I have watched your people offer their gifts willingly and joyously (emphasis mine)."

Remember, as you seek to build Temples, God is looking at the motives of your heart more than your results. When you give, you are primarily giving back to God what He's already given to you. He's looking for people who will give generously to these construction projects currently going on worldwide. I truly believe that if you give with the best intentions and knowledge available at the time, God will never fault you for misused funds. He will still reward you. The people who mishandle the money will be held responsible. And I also believe, consistent with His nature, He will still redeem your gift somehow, providing for the cause for which you sent it.

If you begin giving to a ministry, an orphanage, a child, or even a specific building project, and at some point you want to know for sure how you're money is being used, the best way to find out is to visit the ministry you support. Go and see the work for yourself. When I visited the work being done in Haiti and India, the ministry efforts blew me away. I saw dozens of orphanages with thousands of children who are being taken care of, receiving an excellent education, including learning English (a vital skill in developing countries). These kids know their purpose. They talk about being arrows and changing their countries for Christ. It was mind-boggling to see such focus and commitment among those so young. After seeing the work, I wanted to give even more.

My best advice? "Do your best and leave the rest." Pray that your money will be used wisely and that God will see it through to accomplish the work for which it was sent.

The "American Dream": *I'm so glad God picked me to live this life in America.* While visiting poverty-stricken countries, this is what I thought. In fact, I still feel this way, but now for different reasons. I used to think, not so long ago, that all of the opportunities and relative wealth God gave me was to bless *me*—for me to use and enjoy. Sure, I felt bad about how others lived. But I was, oh, so thankful for the "luck of the draw" that landed me where I could enjoy the good life in America. I bought into the thinking that He picked me to live in a country where I could shamelessly follow the American Dream. And that's pretty much what I did.

My husband and I used to drive two relatively nice cars, and we had a pretty nice start on a retirement account. We had health insurance, more than enough food, and a few years ago we built a big, beautiful home in the country on two pastoral acres. I dreamed of the financial security of paying off our home quickly, acquiring a vacation home someday, and being able to travel and hang out at beach resorts during extended vacations. Maybe throw in a nice golf membership during our retirement.

But in the back of my mind, a nagging question began to surface: *Why did God pick me to live this life and not a desperate, poverty-stricken one?* When I looked around at all the intense suffering and lost dreams in this world, where my brothers and sisters in Christ were born into circumstances beyond their control, I thought, *why isn't that me? And why doesn't somebody do something?*

And then one day I realized . . . *I am somebody.*

On his tour called "The Better Questions," Christian musician Todd Agnew told a story about going to India and seeing all the poverty and how it totally changed him. When he came back from the trip, he asked himself, "Why does God allow this kind of suffering?" After praying and studying the Bible on this topic, he came up with "the better question":

"Why do I allow suffering?"

People get all bent out of shape at God, wondering why He isn't solving world hunger, or giving destitute people homes to live in, or giving people clean water to drink, or keeping people free from curable diseases. The fact is, God's children—you and I—are His ambassadors on this earth. We are His hands, His feet, His heart, His food, and His money. You and I are possibly the only chance this world will ever get to actually see Jesus.

In the delightfully ruinous way that only God can do, He began to completely change my husband's and my thinking about our earthly possessions and our purpose on this earth. One of the penetrating verses He awakened in our hearts at that time was 1 John 3:16–18: "This is how we've come to understand and experience love: Christ sacrificed his life for us. This is why we ought to live sacrificially for our fellow believers, and not just be out for ourselves. If you see some brother or sister in need and have the means to do something about it but turn a cold shoulder and do nothing, what happens to God's love? It disappears. *And you made it disappear.* My dear children, let's not just talk about love; let's practice real love" (MSG).

After my visit to Haiti in 2006, God threw out the challenge to my husband and me, giving us the opportunity to practice real love in a crazy and extravagant manner. We sensed His leading us to sell our newly finished home in order to build an orphanage where Willio could take in even more kids, as well as feed and clothe them properly.

Excuse the overstatement, but this was no small challenge. Aside from being the "American Dream" girl, I have this thing with money. When I say "thing," it's like this. I'm apt to balk when my husband wants to spend $15 on a new rice cooker because the one we bought nine years ago at a garage sale still works. I thrive on the financial security of a chubby savings account, and I love the sanctuary of my own home. Now God was asking us to give up our life's savings in order to save lives in Haiti. When He made it clear that this is what He wanted us to do, the willingness came unexpectedly easy because He had been laying the foundation in our hearts for months, preparing us for that step. Selling our house in 2007 and using most of the equity for orphans has been one of the most amazing, rewarding, and wonderful experiences of our lives, offering our very best to God for the very "least of these" in a way that truly cost us something.

Since that time, we've also gotten more serious about investing in arrows with monthly support. We now help support eight different people of all ages, each in different ministries around the globe. It is so exciting to get their monthly updates, letting us know how our financial assistance is changing lives on four continents. In recent years, we've also developed the practice of investing in teens we know who are going on mission trips. I love hearing about how God uses those trips to nudge them into lifetime service for the Kingdom!

Lest you misunderstand, this is not a guilt-induced message, imploring you to go out, sell all your earthly possessions, take a vow of poverty, and disappear in a secluded monastery. Although, if you're like me, some days, under the pressure of maintaining my inbox, that sounds pretty tempting. I fully understand that God has not called everyone to sell off the farm like we did, nor would it be wise in most cases for a developing family. But this is the part God asked us to play, based on our circumstances and His will for us. And even with that, we still own a nice car, and we're still toting enough household belongings to deck out a small country. I certainly wouldn't turn down a beach vacation under the right circumstances. But just the same, God is going to ask your family to do your part somehow, just like He did with us . . . if you are listening.

Start with One

I recently read some statistics that tell me that we're not "getting" this in American Christianity—that more blessed means more responsibility. At least 85 percent of all church activities and funds are directed toward the internal operations of the congregation, such as staff salaries, utility expenses, and Sunday school materials.[3] Add building funds to that, and you can see why it's reported that the average amount of money going overseas from American churches is only two percent.[4] What's wrong with this picture? The Church of the richest country in the world spending two percent on *the mission*! Sadly, I believe the state of church giving is only a reflection of where our hearts are individually.

God did not give me this financial blessing to keep for myself. He gave it to me because He trusts me to use it for furthering His Kingdom. He trusts that I will take my small lunch and let Him use it to feed multitudes of hungry hearts and stomachs. He's very clear about failure to use His money for its intended purposes in James 5: "This treasure you have accumulated will stand as evidence against you on the day of judgment. For listen! Hear the cries of the field workers whom you have cheated of their pay. The wages you held back cry out against you. The cries of the reapers have reached the ears of the Lord Almighty" (verses 3b–4).

This earth is not our home. It's more like a stay in a temporary hotel room. Why would we invest a ton of money into something that we're not going to stay in permanently—something that's really not ours to keep? But when we invest in *the mission*—when we invest in shaping and sending arrows—then we begin to lavishly decorate our future lasting home.

How many of us, if we're honest, could find the money to make a difference for at least one? If we all helped just one, it would add up enough to make the world a better and less hostile place—and practically teeming with arrows. But many of us are donning our cozy PJs and slippers, relaxing in our comfy recliners in front of our cable TV, snacking on chips, sipping a nice cold glass of clean water, and waiting for God to do something.

Team Effort

As I implore you to get your family started investing in *the mission*, some of you might find Papa's story so inspiring that you only want to support Papa's ministry. Nothing could be further from Papa's heart. I believe his God-given vision of one million arrows was given to benefit all children-shaping ministries—including the ones going on in American homes right now. This vision has to be a team effort if we are ever going to complete *the mission*.

Think about it this way. Papa has a lot of arrows being shaped in India through Hopegivers International, but what about Indonesia? Warm Blankets has arrow-shaping going on in Indonesia. But what about Africa? Kids Alive and Vision Trust have arrows being shaped in Africa. But what about eastern Asia? God's Kids and World Orphans are working there (for a more comprehensive list of specialized orphan ministries, see the resources section).

Another consideration is that different ministries have different needs they minister to, and they are all important. Some feed, some train in lucrative professions, some sharpen for the mission field, some rescue from human trafficking regions, and some fight for justice in countries of oppression. So you see, we can't cover the bases alone—we need to work together. In order for *one million arrows* to become a worldwide reality, we must diversify through different ministries. We must all pray about where God wants us to invest our resources and what ministries fit our family's gifts, desires, etc. But we must all work together to do something.

It's important for you to know that when you invest in kids being raised in most arrow-type ministries (as opposed to primarily humanitarian), you are not usually given the opportunity to correspond directly with a child. There are a couple great reasons for this. Children growing up as arrows have a serious, focused purpose on this earth. It's not practical for an arrow to get distracted (or ruined) by the American lifestyle—a lifestyle that can't help but be communicated through letters, gifts, and pictures. The money received is applied adequately and appropriately to their needs within the scope of their culture. Besides, you can usually get updates from the ministry or the ministry's website about the child(ren) or orphanage you sponsor, and in many cases, you can visit that orphanage. Also understand that in most of the orphanage-type ministries, your money is not supporting only one child, but going for the good of all the children in the home. Anything less would be unfair, not to mention impossible.

Some people might not like the lack of personal interaction. But I've thought about how communicating with the child I'm supporting might seem good for me, but what about for the child? Is it really best for him or her? What if I'm interacting with "my child," and something happens where I can no longer send support? Wouldn't he or she feel rejected? Even though I enjoyed the personal relationship for a time, I can walk away unscathed, but what effects will be left for that child to deal with?

Also, it's important to remember that most arrow-ministry orphanages are like true homes. They are not sterile, loveless environments, harboring emotionally bankrupt kids. They are functioning, loving families, where future arrows enjoy belonging and positive attention. They don't need a new family; they need financial help to pursue *the mission.*

Besides individual sponsorship, I think one of the best ways to get really connected with a ministry and to see how responsibly your money is being used is to get your church, ministry, or group to "adopt an arrow-shaping orphanage." Most ministries would welcome this. Then your group can get involved in a long-term partnership with a specific home or ministry. You'd be amazed at how little money it takes to feed and clothe the kids, and perhaps you could also host special fundraisers for building projects and larger expenses. You can get regular, detailed updates from the orphanage and maybe even schedule annual visits to the orphanage through your church or ministry. Whether it's through financial assistance, prayer, or something else, everybody can get involved and do something to help out with their unique gifts and abilities.

You Can Make a Difference!

In the 1990s, Papa had a chance to visit with Bill Bright, the Campus Crusade Founder who had made Papa the offer to work for him out of Bible college and then supported him with $25 a month for housing. By that time, Papa's church planting ministry had spread to other Asian countries and had multiplied in India to about eight thousand churches and more than three thousand orphans. Dr. Bright shook his head and said, "Thomas, if I knew that my $25 a month could do this much, I would have invested most of my money in this work. I praise God for letting me help you get started in 1960."

In America, we've been blessed beyond measure in ways that other countries cannot imagine. Why has God given us such prosperity and op- portunity? We have the chance to use our God-given resources to gather, sharpen, and launch arrows beyond, and to teach our children to do the same. There are always more children who are awaiting their chance to become arrows in parts of the world where we cannot reach.

"But, young man," we respond. "Do you not realize that there are miles and miles of beach, and there are starfish all along every mile? I can't possibly make a difference!"

But you can! With returns according to the heavenly accounting system (described in Matthew 19:29) of multiplying whatever you give by 100 times, no matter how much or how little you and your family have to offer for sending arrows beyond, *you can make a difference.* Our world is full of orphans who need spiritual parenting, and it starts with just one. It's time to take our bows out of hiding, mend them, and join the workers on the field who are faithfully training children.

There's no lunch too small, no bank account too depleted, that God can't use it to touch multitudes, if we only have willing hearts. Will you make a difference for just one?

PART 3
LAUNCH

Do you think the work of harvesting will not begin

until the summer ends four months from now?

Look around you! Vast fields are ripening all around us

and are ready now for the harvest.

The harvesters are paid good wages,

and the fruit they harvest is people brought to eternal life.

What joy awaits both the planter and the harvester alike!

You know the saying, "One person plants and
someone else harvests."

And it's true. I sent you to harvest where you didn't plant;

others had already done the work,

and you will gather the harvest.

—John 4:35–37

CHAPTER 8

COUNT THE COST

But don't begin until you count the cost. For who would begin construction of a building without first getting estimates and then checking to see if there is enough money to pay the bills? So no one can become my disciple without giving up everything for me.

—Luke 14:28, 33

To have a precious death, we must have lived a precious life. Invest everything you have to locate the costly pearls and hidden treasures, including your time, your talents, your possessions, your children—so that people may not perish but have eternal life.

—M.A. Thomas (Papa)

A few years ago, we built our own home. It didn't take us long into the process to figure out that it was going to be an all-consuming job. After a contractor put up the basic structure, we personally wired every light, outlet, and switch. We threaded what seemed like a mile of plastic tubing for the radiant water heat system through joists in the floors. We drove thousands of nails and screws. We pored over how-to manuals, appliance and window catalogues, and paint swatches. We painted, tiled, added decks, and landscaped. It took a total of four years to finish the job, and during the entire process we put time almost daily into planning the house, working on the house, or talking about the house (I might mention that by the end, our kids were ready to fall on a sword).

When you build your own home, you really have to plan ahead. If you want a quality built structure, you have to carefully calculate the cost from every angle before getting started (and throughout the process), because your house needs to last. You don't cut corners or use cheap materials. You don't try to make the outside look good and neglect what's on the inside. You give it your all—the best of everything you have to offer, so it will be a good investment with promising returns.

We decided early on not to let someone else take over the building process, because then it wouldn't have been done the way we wanted it done. It wouldn't have been our hearts pouring into it. It wouldn't have ended up being the same house that we planned for and envisioned. We did it wholeheartedly because it was ours, and we wanted it to stand the test of time. And, boy, were the results worth it! When it was done, it was everything we'd hoped for—efficient, durable, tranquil, and quite beautiful.

It's the same when we invest in anything of lasting value. The higher the sweat equity, the higher the intrinsic value. And I wonder, if we parents counted the cost up front, putting as much time and energy into the planning and raising of our kids as we did building a lasting, quality home, wouldn't they likely turn out to be rather sturdily and well-built structures, enjoyable to be around, ready to boldly and securely face the storms of life? Wouldn't they be an inviting beacon of spiritual beauty to all who pass by, and thought of as a refuge of peace and joy to all who enter their lives? Wouldn't they be valuable, finished products in the hands of God for engaging *the mission*?

Yes, building a home is like raising a child for God's purposes. And just when all the work is done, and you start getting all comfortable and settled, enjoying the results of your hard work in your amazing, well-built house, you find out that God suddenly wants it back. He wants to use it for a greater purpose. The greatest earthly and eternal value that you and I could ever attach to our kids is to shape them into arrows for God. As you would expect, there is a price to pay. In fact, if we're going to raise our kids to be arrows, and if we are going to send arrows beyond, it's going to require a precious, yet more than worthwhile price.

Blessing or Responsibility?

Abraham was promised a "dream home"—a family enclosed only by the borders of the world, brimming with his own kids. "I will bless you richly. I will multiply your descendants into countless millions, like the stars of the sky and the sand on the seashore. They will conquer their enemies, and through your descendants, all the nations of the earth will be blessed—all because you have obeyed me" (Genesis 22:17–18).

Abraham had history with God. He knew God's character firsthand, so he believed God's promise about the home. He put everything he had into building that household and legacy through his only son of the promise, Isaac. He didn't hold back anything. It was hard work, but he wanted to be a part of building the home that God assured him would yield such staggering returns—it would bless the entire world.

Then God asked him to put his precious house on the altar. He asked for it back.

Abraham didn't waste any time. He didn't whine that he'd just about finished the hard work of building, never getting to enjoy his new home. He didn't even remind God that He had promised this blessing and dream in the first place. He knew that if God wanted his house back—and all the promises that came with it—He would fulfill the dream some other way. Abraham believed that none of his efforts or sacrifices would be wasted. He put that house right up on the altar, stared his hopes and dreams in the youthful face, drew back the knife, and . . .

Wait! When God saw that the house was not more important to Abraham than the One who gave it, He gave it back. In fact, by offering up the thing that meant the most to Abraham, his only son, God gave it all back. Abraham got to keep the house (Isaac) *and* the dream (countless offspring). This is not to say that God will always give back what we lay on the altar. Part of the sacrifice is the not knowing. But truly what He gives in return will be greater than anything we give up.

What is the "Isaac" of your heart—that gift or dream from God that you treasure most? Your kids? Your possessions? Your time? Your money? Are you willing to lay your "Isaac" on the altar to see it come back to life, bigger and better than you ever dreamed possible?

When God asked Abraham to sacrifice all his future dreams and plans on the altar, he obeyed without question. There was only one way this was possible. Abraham knew if he decided to trust God, willingly offering up his last and only hope—his most precious treasure—that he would be given the grace to let it go. He still believed that God would provide.

"What will it cost me to shape and send arrows?" we ask. "What will it cost my kids if they should choose to become arrows?"

In a country that's often hostile toward Jesus and His followers, Papa takes this question seriously. He knows that he's preparing young people for a dangerous calling. They must be ready to face anything. In addition to their regular studies, Papa works through several questions with them as part of his Bible training and spiritual accountability:

- ↪ Are you reading through the Bible every year?
- ↪ Are you fasting and praying?
- ↪ Are you sharing the Gospel with others?

➤ Will you stay in *the mission* and not run away?

➤ Are you willing to die for the cause of Christ—to be faithful until death?

No matter how you slice it, being an arrow, shaping arrows, or sending arrows is costly for everyone involved. For Papa and other arrow shapers, the cost is steep: they give up daily lives, earthly ambitions, material comforts, and in countries like Papa's where Christians are persecuted, sometimes it costs their very lives. But the sacrifice required for the sake of *the mission* is really the same for you and me as it is for them. It's a total letting go of our worldly ambitions and selfish interests, exchanging them for new goals and priorities. It's placing all our hopes and dreams on the altar next to Isaac, waiting for God to resurrect them into something far beyond our wildest dreams. As Andrew Murray reminds us, "Consecrated training requires complete devotion in daily life."[1] So then it is day-by-day devotion, giving up of pride, convenience, popularity, laziness, materialism, and indifference. It's making all our God-given resources—all we have and all we are—mobilized and ready to be used for *the mission. It is dying to self.*

For the most part, this dying to self is a foreign concept to many of us today, myself included. Americanized Christianity promises all the blessings and requires practically none of the responsibilities and sacrifices of authentic, surrendered biblical faith. How well would our version of "committed faith" last in Haiti, where many believers don't have enough money for food, let alone shoes? Or in China, where people are imprisoned for years and put in slave factories for preaching the Gospel or for meeting in homes to worship God? Or how about Pakistan, where individuals are disowned by their families, tortured, or put to death just for owning a Bible or speaking the name of Jesus Christ? If we cannot promote our American version of living by faith in places like Haiti, or China, or Pakistan, we should not promote it here. In other words, there's a cost for truly serving Jesus no matter where you live, and that is the message by which we should govern our lives and homes.

If we really have to give up so much, it's tempting to ask, "Hey, what's in it for me? What will I gain? Is the price worth it?" Paul encourages us that the payoff will be absolutely worth it. "I once thought all these things were so very important, but now I consider them worthless because of what Christ has done. Yes, everything else is worthless when compared with the priceless gain of knowing Christ Jesus my Lord. I am focusing all my energies on this one thing: Forgetting the past and looking forward to what lies ahead, I strain to reach the end of the race and receive *the prize* for which God, through Christ Jesus, is calling us up to heaven" (Philippians 3:7–14, selected). As my life becomes less about me, I find there *is* something in it for me. My family and I, and all those we reach by choosing to pay a price during our extremely short time on earth, are abundantly rewarded forever.

We are also rewarded now when we see our kids living fulfilled, whole, purposeful lives.

In the story of Abraham, it's important to note that God didn't force the sacrifice. He *invited* Abraham to lay down the best he had to offer. God not only planned to give Isaac back, but also He planned to massively multiply the prize for obedience, both in this life and the life to come. As we pursue *the mission* and the prize, we can't go in blindly. We must always count the cost up front. But if we weigh it out, the cost is truly minimal compared to the gain. What's the payoff? Our families becoming a significant part of Papa's vision—better yet, our families doing our part to complete *the mission*. And as great as the blessings may be here in this life, the rewards awaiting us in our future life with Jesus far surpass our wildest imagination. "No eye has seen, no ear has heard, and no mind has imagined what God has prepared for those who love him" (1 Corinthians 2:9).

The Arrow Pledge

In the late 90s, Papa was diagnosed with late stage cancer and given less than a three percent chance at recovery. Even before his death-sentence,

Papa thought many times that he might be living his last day on earth when he faced grave threats, beatings, and hot pursuits by his persecutors. But Papa wasn't afraid to die. Even when I first met him, he was in the middle of a particularly harrowing season of persecution. I'd never met anyone who wasn't afraid of being persecuted or martyred, but Papa patiently explained his heart's desire to me in his gentle and loving manner. "It would be the greatest privilege if God should count me worthy to die for Him. That is my prayer, that He would not take me home any other way." And this is the mentality he models to his students—both his own children and his orphans.

In his book *Seeking Peace*, Johann Christof-Arnold writes, "Like anyone else, Martin Luther King must have been afraid of dying, yet he radiated a deep calm and peace. Here was a man with no doubts as to his mission, and no crippling fears about the cost of carrying it out. 'No man is free if he fears death,' he told the crowd at a civil rights rally in 1963. 'But the minute you conquer the fear of death, at that moment you are free . . . I submit to you that if a man hasn't discovered something that he will die for, he isn't fit to live.'"[2]

I love the "Arrow Pledge" that Papa came up with for his Bible college graduates. Well, actually, Papa calls it the "Martyr's Pledge," but which one would you be more inclined to talk your kids into reciting? Luckily, Papa doesn't have to talk anyone into anything—his Bible students have chosen to pursue *the mission* because they *want* to become arrows—at all costs. Every graduate recites "The Pledge" before receiving his or her diploma:

> *I take a stand to honor the Lord Jesus Christ with my hands, to serve all*
> *mankind.*
> *I take a stand to honor the Lord Jesus Christ with my feet,*
> *to spread the Gospel to all the ends of the earth,*
> *no matter the cost.*
> *I take a stand to honor the Lord Jesus Christ with my lips,*

by proclaiming the Good News to all who hear,
     and by edifying the body of Christ.
I take a stand to honor Jesus Christ with my mind,
     as I meditate upon His Word.
I give my earthly treasures and all that I possess
     to follow the way of the cross.
I commit to love my family, orphans, widows, lepers,
     the wealthy, and the poor,
the way that Christ loved the church.
I surrender my will and life to His will and life.
I commit to the service of the Lord by being
     a good steward of my time.
I surrender my body to the perfect will of Jesus and,
     should my blood be spilled,
may it bring forth a mighty harvest of souls.
I am not ashamed of the Gospel of Christ,
     for it is the power of God unto salvation,
and to everyone who believes.
As a soldier of the cross I stand with
     the Apostle Paul in stating that,
"For me to live is Christ and to die is gain."
Lord Jesus, Thy Kingdom come,
     Thy will be done on earth as it is in heaven.
I love my country and my fellow citizens,
     and I claim my country for Christ. [3]

Hmmm ... raising young people who are so serious about their commitment to Christ that they're willing to show His love, even when it costs them everything—even unto death. How powerful is that?

No more than teenagers, three of Papa's orphan boys were once tested in their Pledge with the fiery furnace of persecution. As a large group of anti-Christians closed in on them at a train station, planning to beat them to death, the young men believed that they were about to give up their lives.

One of the young men took a pen out and wrote on his arm, "I am not only ready to suffer for Christ, I am ready to die for Him." As soon as he finished, he passed the pen and the other two did the same. They thought that, after they were martyred, someone would see their dead bodies, read their arms, and know that they didn't die cowards.

As soon as they wrote these words on their arms, courage mounted in their hearts, and all their fear vanished. Their youthful dreams came back to life as they realized *this was their mission*. There was no greater privilege than to be counted worthy to die for Jesus. When their oppressors put them through the fire of persecution, however, they lived to tell about it. They were beaten, but not killed. Emerging from the flames, they came out unburned and singe-free. I'm sure there were four of them that left the fire together that day. To this day, Papa told me that these men are serving the Lord wholeheartedly in various ministries, none of them afraid to live out costly faith.

People like these are described in Revelation 12:11: "They overcame [Satan] by the blood of the Lamb and by the word of their testimony; they did not love their lives so much as to shrink from death" (NIV). When I think about it, it's no less than what God required of His own Son. And it's no less than the kind of commitment He wants from our families as well.

The Price of Truth

What is our fiery furnace? What price will we and our kids have to pay for our devotion to Christ? For most of us, it's subtle, but it's still there.

When my daughter was in seventh grade, she let me read a report she was working on for science class. I was shocked to see her paper include quotes from a textbook supporting inaccuracies from the theory of evolution, as if she believed them herself. She knew better.

"What's up with your quotes?"

"Well, my teacher told me to do it like this," my straight-A student explained, "and if I don't, I'll get a bad grade."

I grabbed my Bible and opened it up to Daniel 3, and had her read the story about the three young men of God who refused to bow down to worship the king's idol. The king was furious when he heard this: "Is it true, Shadrach, Meshach, and Abednego, that you refuse to serve my gods or to worship the gold statue I have set up? I will give you one more chance. If you bow down and worship the statue I have made when you hear the sound of the musical instruments, all will be well. But if you refuse, you will be thrown immediately into the blazing furnace. What god will be able to rescue you from my power then?"

Shadrach, Meshach, and Abednego replied, "O Nebuchadnezzar, we do not need to defend ourselves before you. If we are thrown into the blazing furnace, the God whom we serve is able to save us. He will rescue us from your power, Your Majesty. But even if he doesn't, Your Majesty can be sure that we will never serve your gods or worship the gold statue you have set up" (verses 14–18).

After she finished reading, I could already see the conviction on her face, but I asked the questions anyhow, as we point-driving parents are prone to do. "So, help me relate this to your science paper situation. In this account, who is the king most like?"

"My science teacher."

"The young men?"

"Me."

"And how does the command he gave them compare to your situation?"

"He tried to make them do something against their beliefs."

"And what is your fiery furnace?"

"Getting a bad grade," she sounded completely annoyed by this time, directing her frustration at me.

I actually left it at that and didn't force her to change her paper or even check to see what she decided. It was time for her to start developing her own strength in holding to personal convictions, and I didn't want to always think for her. That wouldn't teach her to listen to the Holy Spirit. I knew if she made the wrong choice, the Holy Spirit would teach her more than a nagging mother ever could.

After writing this today, I felt curious. Now five years after her "Daniel moment," I asked my daughter—Danielle—what she decided on that paper. She totally remembered the situation. "I did the right thing, Mom."

These days, she enthusiastically describes situations where she stands up for her beliefs in school, even when she is ridiculed by other students or teachers. She's come a long way in standing against her culture by applying many years of at-home Bible training. She now says she would be willing to walk through a fiery furnace rather than deny her God. I pray she's right.

The Price of Possessions

In the way God does, He began preparing us for selling our home months before He actually showed us it was time. Three months before I went to Haiti on my first ever mission trip, and even before I knew anything about Haiti or that I would be going, Shucks and I were finishing up our new lawn one day. Leaning over our rakes on a little break, we began discussing a strange coincidence. We discovered we'd both had the sense in recent days that God was telling us individually it was time to start detaching our hearts from our home. We had no reason to even think that way, and we knew it was significant since we'd both had that impression. Over the months that followed, that theme showed up several times for both of us, especially while reading our Bibles, until we were convinced that God was doing something with our home, but just what or when, we didn't know.

Three months later, I arrived a couple days early in the Dominican Republic to wait for my Haiti mission team. Staying alone in a small, family-owned hotel by the beach, trying to get in a much-needed mental break, I had plenty of time to dive into some great reading material I'd brought along for the trip. Since my parents freaked out about my being alone outside the country, I buried some pepper spray in the recesses of my checked luggage. Did you know you can actually clear out everyone in a small hotel for more than four hours if you test a shot of pepper spray in your room? Oops.

The reading material I brought along for my mini-vacation was a book by Steven James, *Sailing Between the Stars: musings on the mysteries of faith*. Steve's a fellow writer and a good friend of mine. I love his writing and teaching style, so I wanted to check out his new book. I was on the beach those two days before entering Haiti, minding my own business, when I read the following words:

> As they were walking along someone said to Jesus, "I will follow you no matter where you go." But Jesus replied, "Foxes have dens to live in, and birds have nests, but I, the Son of Man, have no home of my own, not even a place to lay my head" (Luke 9:57–58).
>
> "I'll follow you wherever you go," we tell Jesus.
>
> "I have no home," he says. "Will you follow me to the place where you don't either?"
>
> The Quaker author Thomas R. Kelly noted that as God works in our lives, we become less attached to the world and yet, at the same time more concerned for the world: "He plucks the world out of our hearts, loosening the chains of attachment. And He hurls the world into our hearts, where we and He together carry it in infinitely tender love." Somehow Christians should be both more in love with the world and less in love with the world than anyone else.
>
> "Sell what you have and give to those in need," said Jesus. "This will store up treasure for you in heaven! Wherever your treasure is, there your heart and thoughts will be also" (Luke 12:33–34). I think that within these words is an invitation for us to ask not

only the self-evident question, "Where is my treasure?" but also the much more important question, "Where is my heart?"

Zing.[4]

The Ultimate Price

Most of our children who are trying to live out their faith in their unbelieving culture are facing daily battles similar to my daughter's. Compared to the struggles of many believers worldwide, these battles are relatively small. But even in America, some are paying the price with their jobs such as seen in the Ben Stein movie, *Expelled: No Intelligence Allowed*, and others are even paying with their very lives. One of my favorite testimonies is that of Rachel Scott, a victim of the Columbine shootings in the spring of 1999. Excerpted and retold from various passages in her book, *The Journals of Rachel Scott*,[5] her testimony details the greatest cost of surrender:

> Cute. Bubbly. Outgoing. That's how people describe me, which is great if it factors into my dream of becoming famous. Yep, I tell my dad that someday, he's going to see my smiling face on Oprah! I plan to use my fame to make a difference in this world because I want my life to count.
>
> I'm Rachel Joy Scott, seventeen years old, and I'm pretty much a normal teenager, except that I'm a Christian. It's not easy being a Christian, especially when you take that "What would Jesus do?" question seriously, because being a Christian means you always have to do the hard thing—be honest, forgiving, kind, and say no to some of the stuff your friends are doing.
>
> Talking to God—well, I prefer writing to Him—is really how I get the courage and energy to live for Jesus on a day-to-day basis. I've discovered that I can just talk to God like I talk to anyone else. I can make Him smile, laugh, and even cry.
>
> Last year I started going to this really cool youth group. I learned that being a Christian means being like Christ—not

just saying and doing good things, but really knowing God. Once all that started to sink in, I wanted to know God like never before. It became the most important thing to me—even more than becoming famous. Suddenly, I wanted to become the same girl at school that I was at youth group, and I wanted people to see Jesus when they looked at me. I wanted to be a "make-a-difference, love-the-world-and-turn-the-tide" kind of Christian. Not a wimpy, no big deal, politically-correct-and-don't-make-waves kind of Christian. I wanted to start a chain reaction . . .

On April 20, 1999, during lunch break at Columbine High School, Rachel Scott was challenged with these beliefs when she was faced with a pivotal question. After being shot three times in the legs and stomach by one of her classmates, he pressed the cold metal barrel of his handgun against her scalp, "Do you believe in God?"

"You know I do," she answered unflinchingly.

"Then go be with him," he said, shooting her fatally in the head.

Paradoxically, Rachel's dreams came to life through her death. She became famous worldwide, and her tribute even appeared with her dad—on Oprah! Most importantly, she became the love-the-world-and-turn-the-tide kind of Christian. Through her life and death, a chain reaction began as thousands of students and others worldwide listened to her testimony and put their faith in Jesus Christ.[6]

A Pilgrimage of Many

I've discovered something through the process of learning Papa's dream and writing this book: *I am an arrow.* For me, that doesn't mean going to the mission field in person, but instead I'm going with my time, my money, and my gifts and abilities. Even more importantly, I'm investing in my own two arrows to carry on my spiritual heritage. Most days, this is a beautiful, fulfilling, and amazing calling. But some days are overwhelming, tiresome, and discouraging. Sometimes, I get a hankering for a mental break—a vacation. There's always so much to do for my God-given mission and raising my kids for theirs, I feel like I'll never catch up.

Today God reminded me of "Danny and Abigail," a couple who spent time in our home recently during a trip to the U.S. to visit churches. They are both native Israeli Messianic Jews who work tirelessly through Ot-U'Mofet, a sub-ministry of Restorers of Zion, to minister to orphans, widows, and single mothers in Israel according to Psalm 68:5 and James 1:27. "Ot-U'Mofet is taken from Isaiah 8:18," Abigail explains, "and through this ministry we teach how the curse of widowhood can turn into a source of great blessing to the entire body of Christ; how an impossible situation can turn into a 'Sign and a Wonder' of God's ability to restore."[7]

Besides raising funds, they also offer a five-month inner-healing program to help these single women financially, educationally, vocationally, and spiritually. Through this ministry, the couple has seen many women and children restored to purpose and joy in Christ. "Our heart is for these women to see themselves as God sees them. Israel was also a widow but God never forsook her.

"We joined this ministry," Abigail continues, "knowing that when you serve the orphan and widow, you're actually worshiping God. We see all single mothers as widows in many aspects because they are desolate and lonely." The motto of their program, "From Ashes to Victory," describes the way women are rising up from the ashes and moving into victory in all aspects of their lives. "Our workshops teach them to say goodbye to victim mentality, and to stand on their feet as God takes the place of a husband and father."

I also thought about Ralph and Stella, two arrows in their early eighties who have given up real vacations since the 1960s when they moved to Japan as church planters with TEAM. In fact, in 1970 God gave Ralph a vision to plant one hundred churches in Japan, a vision he has steadily worked toward since, despite incredible spiritual opposition. They stay on course, never slipping in an extravagant break. Even when they come home to the States on furlough, they're on a whirlwind schedule, visiting and speaking at churches that support them all over the country.

These friends make incredible sacrifices every day, working hard for *the mission*. I don't think for a second that everyone has to give up vacations, and especially not naps, but these diligent arrows encourage me on those tired days to keep on track and not give up, because an arrow can never waiver or it will lose its path. Once launched, it must unswervingly stay on course until it hits the target.

My target has become, along with Papa's, *one million arrows for God*. Papa and all these others—Danny, Abigail, Ralph, Stella, and Willio—never take breaks from their work. Maybe I shouldn't strive for big, fancy vacations either. At the least, I can never settle for passivity or let up on my part of *the mission*, either in my own life or in how I raise my kids. My real vacation is coming up soon, and it will be decidedly long enough to get rested. Remember, this short experience on earth is the work. Heaven is *the rest*. When we really get that, the price becomes more than worth it. That's why Papa's dad willingly gave up his dreams of having an educated son who would provide for the family so his son could wholeheartedly serve the Lord. Even today if you bring it up, Papa tears up when he tells you about all the sacrifices his parents made to let him follow God's plan for his life. But he will tell you that God was absolutely faithful to his parents for their decision. "I praise God for my dad's decision that day. He made no mistake! He has never regretted his decision nor suffered from it. In fact, he has been abundantly rewarded—far above anything he could imagine—because he gave his first-born to the Lord's work."

"Since God did not spare even his own Son but gave him up for us all, won't God, who gave us Christ, also give us everything else" (Romans 8:32)? God gave the best He had for us, His only Son, Jesus. Abraham gave the best he had for God, his only son, Isaac. Papa gives the best he has for orphans, his everyday life. What are you and I willing to give?

Giving up is about the condition of our hearts, not about living below the poverty line. It's about continually prying our hearts from everything God has given us, making it all available for *the mission*, lest it become so important that it strangles God's individual dreams for us. His dreams are so much grander than what we now hold in our hands. Let us build our treasures in heaven, where they will never get stolen or worn out.

"I plead with you to give your bodies to God," Paul exhorts us. "Let them be a living and holy sacrifice—the kind he will accept. When you think of what he has done for you, is this too much to ask? Don't copy the behavior and customs of this world, but let God transform you into a new person by changing the way you think. Then you will know what God wants you to do, and you will know how good and pleasing and perfect his will really is" (Romans 12:1–2). As I read that verse, I sometimes think that dying for Jesus might be easier than living for Him. Living for Him requires a slow, painful dying to self process every single day.

"Is God asking me to give up my home?" we ask. No, certainly not. He wouldn't do that.

He's asking for more. But never more than He has already given up for us.

Hold it all loosely.

Use it all for His glory.

He wants *everything.*

CHAPTER 9

KEEP YOUR EYES ON THE PRIZE

I am focusing all my energies on this one thing: forgetting the past and looking forward to what lies ahead, I strain to reach the end of the race and receive the prize for which God, through Christ Jesus, is calling us up to heaven.
—Philippians 3:13–14

Christ, the ultimate investment counselor, says, "Don't ask how your investment will be paying off in just thirty years. Ask how it will be paying off in thirty million years." Every day is an opportunity to buy up more shares in His Kingdom.
—Randy Alcorn[1]

Being an arrow is a lot like signing up for *Fear Factor*. You know there's going to be a lot of suspense, some fun and interesting challenges, some really hard mental and physical obstacles, and of course, plenty of fear as you're stretched way out of your comfort zone.

Shucks and I put on a *Fear Factor* for our church's youth group a couple years ago. Some of the favorite challenges we came up with were "bobbing for bananas," which consisted of sticking their begoggled faces into a vat of cooked oatmeal amid big slimy night crawlers, to grab a banana in their teeth; "slurping guppies" by drinking down a full glass of water containing several slippery, swimming, squirming guppies; and of course, ingesting a smorgasbord of delectable food items—delectable to Shrek at least.

Our participants were nervous, intimidated, grossed out, and at times very, very afraid, but they still competed eagerly. Why? We offered a hundred bucks to the lucky winner—a lot of dough to a kid. We knew that in order for them to willingly subject themselves to the difficult challenges ahead, the prize had to be worth it.

Paul had a lot to say about the prize for those participating in *the mission*:

- ↪ It's huge and never-ending (1 Corinthians 9:24–27).
- ↪ Focusing on it will keep you from giving up before you finish (Philippians 3:12–14).
- ↪ Getting caught up in temporary gain or the cares of this world can disqualify you from receiving it (2 Timothy 2:4–7).
- ↪ It awaits those who finish *the mission* well (2 Timothy 4:5–8; 2 John 1:8–9).

Keeping our eyes on the prize continuously will get us through those difficult, overwhelming, doubtful, scary, trying days on this earth while we're trying to ready and engage ourselves and our kids for *the mission*. I can tell you now that you're going to get discouraged at times, wondering if your methods are even working with your kids, especially in this culture. But remember that you cannot fully know the results until later. You may have setbacks or even temporary defeats, but that is not an indication of the outcome or the end of the story. Losing a battle here or there is not the same as losing the war. It's days like these we must focus on our Kingdom goal, keeping it in the forefront of all our thoughts and decisions.

I used to think that focusing too much on heavenly things was a lame escape from this world. But Paul exhorts us in Colossians 3:1–2, "Since you have been raised to new life with Christ, *set your sights on the realities of heaven*, where Christ sits at God's right hand in the place of honor and power. *Let heaven fill your thoughts*. Do not think only about things down here on earth" (emphasis mine).

Along with getting excited about our future resurrected life of rest, riches, and intimate relationship with Jesus, we can also focus on the more immediate gratification—souls won for the Kingdom. "After all," Paul exhorts, "what gives us hope and joy, and what is our proud reward and crown? It is you! Yes, you will bring us much joy as we stand together before our Lord Jesus when he comes back again. For you are our pride and joy" (1 Thessalonians 2:19–20).

On my trips to other countries where arrows are being shaped by the locals and sent by the foreigners, I've decided that it could only be continuous thoughts of the prize that motivate these hard working people to stay focused, giving themselves completely to their part in *the mission*. It's the only way they could possibly survive. They have sacrificed so much more than I can even imagine. Giving up my home now seems like such a small thing.

One young arrow couple, "David and Anita," decided to take on the job nobody else will touch, literally. As if taking care of unwanted children wasn't enough, they operate an orphanage in India that takes in orphans with AIDS. In India, nobody—not even Christians—wants to touch or help anyone with AIDS, especially orphans. In fact, this couple gets referrals frequently from prominent "Christian" ministries that don't want to take care of these kids for fear they'll spread infection or get a negative stigma from society. Sadly, whenever a ministry stops by David's orphanage and drops off a sick kid, they don't even offer any money to help provide for the child.

Taking care of AIDS kids is a difficult enough job when you don't have financial and social roadblocks. But in countries like India where you do, it's next to impossible. David can't let any of his neighbors know about his kids or he will get evicted from his neighborhood. He frequently reminds the kids not to talk about their health issues with anyone, and he has to hide all their medications in case of unannounced visitors. Seeing how covert his home is reminded me of the Jews hiding out during the Holocaust.

All the kids have a special, individual diet for their particular stages and manifestations of AIDS. This means catering each meal to each child's individual needs. Finding help is also challenging, because no one wants to touch the children. David has finally turned to his last resort, hiring prostitutes with fairly advanced cases of AIDS to help him take care of the children. But they don't usually live long and then he's left short-handed once again.

As you might expect, without government aid or community help, the cost of medicine and hospital treatment is over the top. Frequently, one of the kids has to be secretly transported to the hospital. In addition, every child needs special medicines daily and weekly. You would never know, talking with David and Anita, that their lives are so hard. They don't complain. They wear smiles. Even when their medicine closet and pantry are nearing empty, they don't ask for money. They pray.

The most amazing thing to me was how happy these kids are—more so than many of their healthy counterparts. David told us his secret. His motto for this home and for his life is "laugh, love, live." He is committed to providing these three gifts as much as possible for the kids during their limited days on earth. And the "live" part of the equation is that, though their young lives are being cut short, he might teach them how to obtain eternal life through Jesus Christ. The bright smiles they beamed as we watched them clap and sing upbeat praise songs reflected amazing hope and joy in their somewhat restored childhood.

David and Anita are making such amazing sacrifices every day. Not only have they renounced the comforts they might have sought in another profession, but also they are truly giving up their lives 24/7 and being Jesus to the "least of these." They are feeding, clothing, sheltering, and loving the most unlovable and despised of their whole society. How do they do it? What gets them through the days? They focus on bringing children "home," keeping in mind their time is short to make a difference before the start of their nice, long vacation.

The second couple I met is equally inspiring. Dan and Viji were both born in India, but Dan ended up living in the United States from the age of fifteen until about the age of thirty-five. During his adult years in the States, he worked for a prominent financial institution and got promoted to a regional vice-president.

After attaining the American Dream—the large house, pool, BMW, six figure income, paid vacations, retirement plan, even helicopter rides to some of his appointments—Dan felt the dissatisfaction growing in his soul.

"What do you want me to do, Lord?" he finally asked.

He felt the Lord tell him that He wanted him to sell his house (do we see a theme here?), quit his job, and move back to India to start an orphanage for young girls. In India, young girls are particularly vulnerable to exploitation, with sex trafficking and slavery of all kinds. Young boys can typically fare better for themselves.

It was one of the toughest decisions Dan ever made. He liked his life in the States. It was easy. He was comfortable. But God had a way of making him quite uncomfortable until he finally agreed.

"For the first couple years, I thought I made the biggest mistake of my life," Dan remembers. "I thought I ruined my family's lives. Everything was so hard, and none of us were used to life in India. America was the only life my kids had ever known."

But over time, when they were able to settle into the culture and get the home going, their hearts got engaged in the meaningful impact they were making in lives. Now, many years later, Dan and Viji believe without a doubt that they did the right thing, and they have seen God do so many miracles, both in their lives and in the rescued girls' lives.[2]

Both of these couples have given up a lot of comforts in this world in order to pursue *the mission.* They've made untold sacrifices. But they're building a far greater, lasting treasure, both in the lives of kids, and in the future world.

Hold the Ropes

William Carey coined an expression during his lifetime: *Expect great things from God, attempt great things for God.*

An Englishman, known as "the father of modern missions," Carey had a profound impact on India. He moved to Calcutta in 1792, at the age of thirty-two, after starting up the Baptist Missionary Society in England. During his lifetime, he translated and printed the Bible in whole or in part into forty-four languages and dialects.[3]

Before Carey committed himself physically to the mission field, he and three members of his Society listened to a visiting missionary describe the vast need for the Gospel in eastern India, where millions of hungry souls waited. His three friends looked at him and one said, "We see that there is a gold mine in India, and it is as deep as the center of the earth. Who will dare to explore it?"

"I will go," Carey told them. "I will descend this mine; but you must not forget to firmly hold the ropes!"

What were the ropes Carey referred to? The continuous supply of money and resources—the lifelines—he would need to embark on and complete an effective mission in order to get the prize. Carey was willing to descend into the unknown dark of the mine, because he'd heard about the amount of gold waiting to be harvested. He also knew he'd recover a treasure far greater this way than any he'd find up on the safe surface. He believed Jesus when He said, "The Kingdom of Heaven is like a treasure that a man discovered hidden in a field. In his excitement, he hid it again and sold everything he owned to get enough money to buy the field—and to get the treasure, too! Again, the Kingdom of Heaven is like a pearl merchant on the lookout for choice pearls. When he discovered a pearl of great value, he sold everything he owned and bought it" (Matthew 13:44–46).

The work of an arrow is never complete because the gold and treasure is always there, waiting for someone to persist in digging it up. Many ministries and individuals worldwide today are training workers for the spiritually dark places where the buried treasure lies in wait. Many workers are sacrificing every single day to find the gold. We can't just lower them halfway down and let go of the rope, abandoning them. *The mission* would die. They need help bringing the gold to the surface, until there is no more. We must commit to hold the rope while the workers descend the deep shafts of the mine, collecting the gold. As time goes by, we must faithfully support and pray for them.

God's Blessings Now

I really love how God gives back. I'm not talking about winning the lotto or finding out Aunt Agnes left me a fortune. I'm talking about a loving Father reaching down to provide for me as His child and to reassure me with surprise life gifts in response to my generosity and sacrifices for *the mission*. Papa once told me that when you take care of the orphans, God takes care of you. I've discovered for myself that Papa is right.

The year before we sold our house, we planted over thirty-five trees when we landscaped. One of the trees I was particularly excited about was a sweet cherry. I'd always wanted a cherry tree, and we somehow came across a variety that is sweet, yet would grow in a climate agreeable to polar bears. The nursery we bought it from, as well as other cherry tree owners in the area, all told us the same thing, "Don't expect cherries the first two years at least." At the time, I didn't know this news would be so disappointing.

As soon as our house went under contract for sale in mid-May, I lamented. "Lord, I really wanted cherries. Now I'll never know what they're like." Sounds trivial, I know. But this is how I felt.

About a week later, my little cherry tree blossomed. Not just a few blossoms either. Its small frame was loaded with delicate, pink flowers. Two months later, not long before leaving our house to the new owners, we harvested exactly enough cherries to make one plump cherry pie!

Some people would think that was coincidence or that I was silly to worry about cherries when the world is full of much bigger problems. But those cherries demonstrated God's love, compassion, and attention to the small details of our lives. To us, they were His personal house-parting gift.

The week before we moved out in August, we went for our last walk around the neighborhood. Half way home, it began to rain lightly, which sort of matched our mood that day. We grieved the loss of our dream home and battled the insecurity we felt in giving it all up. Walking hand in hand, we prayed out loud together about our future.

"Lord," I said, "you know how much we love this house and neighborhood, but we love your orphans even more. We hope you will take the money and multiply it a hundred times . . ."

"Why not a thousand times?" Shucks cut in.

"OK, . . . a thousand times . . . for your Kingdom. And Lord, this is a big deal to us. We've never done anything this crazy. This is a lot of security we're giving up. Please give us another reassurance that you'll take care of us if we give all this up for you and your children."

Tears fell from heaven, it seemed, mixing with the ones on our cheeks.

A half-mile later, as we rounded a corner to head home, we stopped in awe. There, perfectly framing our home was the most vivid double

rainbow either of us had ever seen in our lives. It was big, it was bold . . .
it was ours. We knew it, without a doubt. We prayed God would leave it
there long enough for us to get pictures, so we'd never forget. And He did.
We got pictures in our yard, down the street, and across the field, our joy
overflowing as we ran from place to place, snapping away (we also got a
few raised eyebrows from the neighbors).

It was our personal reassurance—another prize from heaven—and it's
been one of the most precious memories and reassurances to us since. All
this is to say that God cares about the things I care about—and the things
you care about. Even cherries. And His presence is never more pronounced
than when we're taking risks for Him, living sacrificially and surrendered.
When we show up to do our part, He leads us into the great adventure.

I wish I could tell you all of the other miracles God did surrounding
the sale of our house, but we would practically need another book. But just
remember, whenever you give something up for God, He gives so much
more in return. As I write this, it hasn't been that long since we sold, but we
know without a doubt that He's going to take care of us beyond our wildest
imagination. Our prayer is that He gives even more financial blessings, not
for us, but so that we can invest in even more arrows. Maybe someday we'll
become a clearinghouse for God's money!

If you ask me, the most worthwhile prize in all of this is that we're
teaching our children to invest in God's Kingdom and to care about
sending arrows. As part of the training process, we're modeling for our
kids how to cherish the opportunity to give to *the mission*. We want
our kids to grow up putting their time, talents, and money into eternal
investments, so that their hearts will follow close behind.

Guaranteed ROI

Randy Alcorn says, "I'm convinced the greatest deterrent to giving is
this: the illusion that this earth is our home. When Jesus warns us not to

store up treasures on earth, it's not just because wealth might be lost; it's because wealth will always be lost. No exceptions."[4]

In light of the downturn in the economy, where people have lost so much of their savings and retirement, this thought rings so true. I've thought many times how much better—and safer—it would have been had we invested our lost savings in Heavenly Bonds. If we lived a "Treasure Principle Life," maybe we'd be more motivated to keep giving and not to worry so much about earthly accumulation, security, and wealth. In fact, I've come up with nine good reasons—all prizes for me—why I should give of my money and resources for shaping and sending arrows *now*, while I'm still alive:

9. I won't be in danger of God's warnings against the rich (Matthew 19:24; James 5:1–5).

8. I can't take it with me, but I can send it on ahead (Job 1:21, Luke 12:33).

7. Whatever I send ahead will never get lost, stolen, or wear out (Matthew 6:19–20).

6. The less stuff I own, the less it owns me. That's less I have to take care of, worry about losing, and spend even more money to maintain (Ecclesiastes 5:10–15).

5. The resources I give to make and send arrows will result in many, perhaps thousands, being saved, as well as bring about everlasting friendships (Luke 16:9).

4. My future home will get nicely decked out before I even get there.

3. My kids won't fight over what I don't leave them.

2. My return on investment will yield a hundred times the amount given (Matthew 19:29).

1. It's one way that little ol' me is totally able to make a significant contribution to *the mission*, and to be a part of changing the world (Matthew 28:18–20).

Two people who keep their eyes on the prize more than anyone I've ever met are Papa and his son, Sam. If either of them sees someone in need of something they have or are wearing, they'll take it off right then and give it to them. Papa raised Sam to be this same way, partly by example and partly by coercion (sometimes referred to by parents as "training").

A couple years ago, a newly acquired orphan needed a heart operation, and the doctor required an immediate blood donor. Several people in the ministry volunteered to be tested for the proper blood type, among them Sam. As it happened, out of all the volunteers, Sam, president over one of the largest Christian ministries in India, was the only one with the correct blood type.

"The devil asked me, 'You're doing all this for a child who doesn't even have a mom or dad? Why would you do this for a street kid? You haven't even done this for your own kid. Who will thank you? Who's going to care?'

"At that moment, I answered back to him, 'God cares. He's a Father to the fatherless. He will thank me someday.'

"Some time later," Sam continues, "while visiting one of the orphanages, I saw a kid lying down on the couch. This kid comes over to me, opens his shirt, and reveals a scar on his chest and says, 'Sam, sir, thank you very much for giving your blood to me. I have accepted Jesus as my Lord and Savior, and I want you to baptize me.'

"That was the best thing I could possibly hear. That's why we do this."

It's so like God to orchestrate such an example of servant leadership by requiring the busy, influential leader to stop and humbly offer his very lifeblood for one of his orphans. At that moment, it was only the blood of the leader and earthly spiritual father that could preserve a precious boy's life under his care—the life that was once considered dispensable and unworthy by others.

Sam gave his blood to save a child's life, which resulted in the child being saved through Christ's blood for eternity. God gave Sam the opportunity to be an earthly example of Jesus' extravagant heavenly love and sacrifice. For him there was no greater calling—no greater prize—in that moment. And the once unwanted child understood that he was now part of a real family. He realized if he was worthy of Sam's blood, he was worthy of the life-saving blood of Sam's God.

As we focus on the gain—lives saved and treasures stored—our giving will become, in every way and every area of life, extravagant. We are the hands and feet, sometimes the blood, and especially the pocketbook of Christ to a spiritually lost and dying world.

Will our reward be worth it? Recently I checked into the going rate for CDs. Around two lousy percent, whether six months or two years. We could have kept all the money from the sale of our house and invested it at two percent, or with a competent investor, maybe even yielded as much as 15 percent. Or the best scenario, we could have reinvested in more property or built another house, and potentially made up to 100 percent returns if we were hard-working and shrewd about it.

Jesus tells us in Matthew 19:29, "And everyone who has given up houses or brothers or sisters or father or mother or children or property, for my sake, *will receive a hundred times as much in return* and will have eternal life" (emphasis mine). I'm no CPA or financial advisor, but I did the math, and my calculator tells me that anything I give up for God and His work on this earth will yield quite a return for me in the next life. In heavenly ROI, that's about 10,000 percent net profit. And who knows, maybe the interest will compound for eternity!

I don't know if God actually means I'll get a hundred houses in the Kingdom, but I do believe He was telling the truth in principle. Giving up my stuff for Jesus is not really giving up anything. It's investing in a bottomless cup of eternal blessings for every one drop of earthly giving.

Winning the Prize

Almost exactly one year after we sold our house so that the Haiti orphans could get a safe, comfortable home, their dreams came true on a late November day in 2007. Who knows how many hundreds of kids will be raised in that new home to change Haiti for Christ? I can't tell you how giddy with excitement we felt that day. It really was like winning a great prize!

At one time I was hesitant to tell anyone what we had done or to write about it in this book because of the exhortation in Matthew 6:4: "Give your gifts in secret, and your Father, who knows all secrets, will reward you." But then I thought about it. We didn't invest in the orphanage in Haiti to get anything for ourselves. We are just happy about how many more kids will be rejoicing in heaven because Willio has more room now. And if our story inspires others to give extravagantly to *the mission*, that is all the reward we need.

Who knows how God might use you to change an unwanted child's life? If you decide to make and send arrows, just maybe you'll be shaping and sending the next Billy Graham, Lottie Moon (a famous missionary to China), William Carey, Amy Carmichael, George Muller, or even Papa. The more willing you are to give, the more heavenly the results will be. Consider 2 Corinthians 9:6–14:

> Remember this—a farmer who plants only a few seeds will get a small crop. But the one who plants generously will get a generous crop. You must each make up your own mind as to how much you should give. Don't give reluctantly or in response to pressure. For God loves the person who gives cheerfully. And God will generously provide all you need. Then you will always have everything you need and plenty left over to share with others. As the Scriptures say, "Godly people give generously to the poor. Their good deeds will never be forgotten."
>
> For God is the one who gives seed to the farmer (resources) and then bread to eat (a harvest). In the same way, he will give you many opportunities to do good, and he will produce a great harvest of generosity in you.

Yes, you will be enriched so that you can give even more generously. And when we take your gifts to those (orphans) who need them, they will break out in thanksgiving to God. So two good things will happen—the needs of the (orphans) will be met, and they will joyfully express their thanksgiving to God. You will be glorifying God through your generous gifts. For your generosity to them will prove that you are obedient to the Good News of Christ. And they will pray for you with deep affection because of the wonderful grace of God shown through you (my personal applications to passage in parenthesis).

For less than many of us spend watching movies in a month, or buying lattes, or getting our hair done, we could help shape at least one arrow—one that will make perfect contact with its target. As Papa reminds us, "Today there are many boys and girls like Joseph, abandoned in the wells of death, whom God could place in positions to save nations from their spiritual hunger. Who will help them? Today there are orphans in our care, like Esther, whom God could use to save entire nations from spiritual annihilation. Who will pray for them? Today there are many little ones like Moses, rescued from death and now in our care, whom God could use to lead those held captive by sin into the spiritual Promised Land of eternal life. Who will send them?"

As we raise our own arrows, will you also join me in holding the ropes for others who are mining the gold so we can retrieve the prize together? It's truly worth whatever small, earthly treasures we give up in exchange for so many invaluable, eternal ones. Together we'll finally arrive at our destination—*one million arrows for God*. But why stop there? Perhaps we'll find, as our own families and children perpetuate this vision, that we are only just beginning, and millions of arrows begin soaring in every region and country of the world.

CHAPTER 10

LAND A BULL'S-EYE, CHANGE THE WORLD

. . . The God of our ancestors has chosen you to know his will and to see the Righteous One and hear him speak. You are to take his message everywhere, telling the whole world what you have seen and heard.

—Acts 22:14–15

If you are a Christian, God has saved you for a purpose—to make a difference in your generation. God is calling you to change your world.

—Alvin Reid[1]

Did you know that most movements of God that historians call "great awakenings" have started with young people?[2] Fathers of great faith movements and revivals, such as Jonathan Edwards, John Wesley, William Carey, George Whitefield, George Muller, as well as modern evangelists such as Bill Bright, Billy Graham, Luis Palau, and many others, were mere youths when God called them to join a vision for great change. Throughout the

Bible, we've seen how God frequently used young people to enact serious change on cultures, nations, or even the world at large.

In fact, when God selects His special agents, He doesn't ever measure by appearance, age, experience, or talent; He measures by heart. Joseph, Samuel, David, Esther, Jeremiah, Daniel, Mary—all were but inexperienced young-sters with few human possibilities looming on the horizon when God called them out for a world-impacting Mission Impossible. None of these young people had to wait to grow up to make a difference for their generation or their world.

One of my favorite Bible kid's success stories is Josiah. When Josiah was only eight years old, God put him on the throne of Israel as King, with a great mission in mind for him. At sixteen, when he had matured into a young man, Josiah began seeking his God wholeheartedly on his own, discovering that his purpose was to change a whole nation with truth and justice (1 Kings 13:2). This was especially miraculous from a human standpoint, because based on family heritage; he should have either been wicked or dead. Through his reign, Josiah restored the Temple, tore down hundreds, if not thousands of pagan shrines, eradicated idol worship and witchcraft, and reinstated the Passover with a celebration unlike any the Israelites had ever seen. And it all started with an eight-year-old!

When Josiah's life on earth was over, here's how the Bible described him. "Never before had there been a king like Josiah, who turned to the LORD with all his heart and soul and strength, obeying all the laws of Moses. And there has never been a king like him since" (2 Kings 23:25). God gave Josiah the divine opportunity, and Josiah was faithful to the call of changing his world for the sake of God's Kingdom.

It's no different today. Our sons and daughters are not only the hope of the *future* church—they are the hope of the church *now*. Will the words used to describe Josiah's faithful obedience be the words that describe your children and my children one day?

Will your children change their school for Christ?

How would you feel if your son came home and announced he'd just joined a newly formed club at school . . . for gays? In his sophomore year, Jeremy West ventured out to change his high school by going where no other Christian schoolmates would dare to go. The reason? He wanted to demonstrate God's unconditional love to this group who were often shunned by others, including Christians.

Even though Jeremy's views contradicted those of the gay members of the group, he still earned their respect with his gentle approach. "It's not right for Christians to tell gays, 'You need to stop what you're doing! You need to change!' They don't have the Gospel. They can't change themselves. We need to present the Gospel in love, then let God do the rest."[3]

Jeremy's number one, top priority in pursuing such a radical endeavor was *the mission*. Did he succeed? Absolutely! Mom and Dad West taught their son how to stand alone in a crowd in order to do what Jesus would do, a must for arrow sharpening. Without a doubt, he affected a change in his school in the lives of both believers and unbelievers alike. Who knows how his influence will impact lives for years to come?

Will your children change their culture for Christ?

Jack and Kim Anderson of Denver, Colorado, have raised three kids, all of whom are making a radical difference on their culture. Their oldest daughter, Chloe, has a desire to light up her culture through her love of filmmaking by "producing films that speak Christian truths in ways that are winsome for secular audiences." Her very first film, *Sisterhood*, produced when she was nineteen, was accepted into two secular Film Festivals—the Phoenix Film Festival and the International Student Film Festival in L.A., where it was received quite well by Hollywood filmmakers, winning an award for "Best High School Documentary-Drama."

Now Chloe is studying film at Denver University. "I want to cause people to think and to question the assumptions our relativistic culture has imposed on them. For a world that thinks with its heart, our strategies for shaping culture must shift, and I'd like to be able to capture their hearts and imaginations for Christ. With its enormous potential audience, film seems like a critical area to be focusing on as Christians strategize about reclaiming our culture."[4]

Lately Chloe has been working with 10X Productions on a film, called *The Enemy God*, a true, redemptive story about a young warrior in the Amazon who fears no spirit except the Spirit of God, who he believes to be his enemy. The film has received numerous Film Festival awards, including the Redemptive Storyteller Award, Best Cinematography, and a Best International Film Award in 2008.

Chloe thanks her parents for the opportunities she has in her life today. "From a very young age, they taught me that God was big, that He did big things, and that He expected much out of His people. They also put a very big emphasis on using our talents to serve other people."

Mom and Dad Anderson raised their kids to think God-sized dreams and never to limit what He could do through them, no matter what their ages. Because of that, they have sharpened three arrows who are actively changing their culture for Christ.

Will your children change their country for Christ?

Joe and Jane King of Fountain Inn, South Carolina, had no idea how their lives would be blessed when they brought home their adopted baby boy in 1972. To their delight, Clayton gave his life and future to God in total surrender at the age of fourteen, feeling certain that God was calling him into ministry. From that night on, he began having phenomenal opportunities to speak and preach in many venues, as well as to start a thriving Christian ministry with only a phone and an answering machine in his college dorm room.

Since then, Crossroads Worldwide has united ministries for preaching the Gospel, making disciples, supporting youth and college leaders, and

building community among believers. Eventually, the ministry began putting on hugely successful summer camps for teens, raising over $420,000
for orphan arrows overseas, holding ministry summits, and guiding several
hundred young people on life-changing mission trips to India and Haiti.
Clayton currently speaks to over 200,000 people annually at national
conferences, college campuses, and youth rallies.

When asked who had the most profound effect on his spiritual shaping process, Clayton doesn't hesitate: "My dad, without a doubt. He always
lived out an example in front of me. He was my Sunday school teacher, a
prayer leader in our home, and the godliest man I've ever met. He shaped
me more than anyone else."[5]

Mom and Dad King raised Clayton not to focus on human success,
but to pursue God success—to be completely, courageously surrendered
to *the mission*, willing to take risks. "The worst thing we can do is play
it safe," Clayton says. "People who play it safe never make history. They
die and nobody remembers what they did for God. Revolutionaries—guys
that risk it all—make history. They're the ones who change the course of
humanity."

Will your children change their world for Christ?

Loyd and Renee Teakell of Mooresville, North Carolina, had no idea
just how early in life God would ask them to pull back the bowstring and
release their little arrow, Paula. The real adventure for Paula began when
she went on a two-week mission trip to the Philippines by herself at age
fifteen. Then, as soon as she arrived, she discovered that she was scheduled
to be the main speaker at a three-day youth revival. "I had never preached
before in my life, and I was so scared! But God gave me the words to speak.
By the last night we had 125 kids in attendance."[6]

On this trip, God impressed upon Paula that He wanted her to
move to the Philippines—now—to start a youth ministry in Angeles
City. Paula knew from past conversations that her parents would be

totally against it, partly because she hadn't even graduated yet. But she prayed about it, and when she got home, God had miraculously prepared her parents to say yes—as soon as she got her G.E.D.

In conjunction with learning a difficult Filipino language in only three months and starting a thriving youth ministry, Paula discipled six youth leaders for two years, and she also began raising two abandoned girls, ages nine and ten. Only a kid herself, you can see her plate has been pretty full. "There were many days when I would look around at the tasks before me," Paula says. "I would see all that God was doing, and be in awe that He was using me, a teenager, to do it! It was amazing!"

But there are the "other" days, too. Paula says after times of slow progress, "There are days when I get discouraged and want to give up." But then there have been times when things came together. Once after a visit to the States, Paula went back and was surprised by how much the kids had grown spiritually in her absence; they seemed like different kids! When she expressed her pleasure about their newfound passion for God, they explained, "We are your plants. You planted us and now we're growing!"

Today, Paula stands amazed. "When I look at these youth and see what God has done in them in the past few years, I'm reminded of my purpose and why God sent me here—to train and disciple these kids to go change their world for Jesus."

Mom and Dad Teakell had no idea just how the principles they'd taught their daughter to "always aim higher and never to be satisfied with where you're at" would be tested, not only in her, but also in themselves as they prepared for the cost of releasing their daughter for the mission field.

Home Front Potential

I'll admit, after writing this book and discovering all these amazing stories, I have underestimated what God can do through my kids *now*.

My goals and dreams for my family have been far too small. Sure, I've always tried to do all I could to enrich their life experiences and to make them well-rounded. I've signed them up for piano lessons, musicals and plays, sports teams and camps, arts and crafts classes, and church camps. We've taken them ice-skating, mountain climbing, trout fishing, hot-air balloon riding, snow skiing, and, stupid though it turned out to be, cliff jumping into water fresh off the glaciers. They've exhausted every inch of Disneyworld, traipsed through ancient Mayan ruins in Mexico, jammed to an impressive four-day lineup of their favorite Christian rock groups at the Columbia River Gorge, picked blueberries as big as marbles in the mountains of New Hampshire, and camped with the grizzlies in Grand Teton National Park. In short, they've really had amazing, adventurous, all-American kid lives.

While I was happy for them to pursue all of the normal kid stuff, and it was wonderful for them to become enriched through these experiences, I realize now that it wasn't enough. I don't mean they needed more experiences. It's just that these activities alone would likely produce two girls who still live in a small world comprised of their own desires and dreams, with little thought given to God's dreams for them, or of hurt and sadness in a world without Christ.

As I've begun learning about many kids out there who are doing so many inspiring things, nothing has become clearer to me than this: I have aimed far too low for my kids, and I have not adequately encouraged or readied them to reach their God-given potential. *I have lived as if the world is God's gift to my children, instead of living like my children are God's gift to this world.*

C.S. Lewis once made the point that God is not as offended that we want too much, as He is by the fact that we are satisfied with so little.[7] As parents, we need to think big, dream big, and pray big for the opportunities God might prepare for our children. We can't afford to settle for the world's dreams or definitions of success—they are so small by comparison!

From now on, I don't want children who are just productive members of society. I don't want to encourage my kids to strive after mere happiness either. In the short window of opportunity I have to impact their lives, *I want to raise spiritually fulfilled kids who are productive members of eternity.* And there is only one place to start.

George Barna, author of *Revolutionary Parenting*, reminds us: "When you ponder your life and legacy, what do you think about? My inclination is to focus on grand outcomes—spiritual revolutions . . . major cultural transformations . . . But for so long, I missed the fact that a spiritual revolution that takes place 'out there' is less significant in God's eyes unless I can facilitate one 'in here'—in my own heart, first, and then in the lives of the people who live under the same roof as me. In particular, it is critical that I see such a revolutionizing faith redefine the lives of my children. My obsession should be on the spiritual growth curve of each of my kids . . . If I am going to be aggressive about something, it should be in how I intentionally shape the lives of my children."[8]

Maybe as you face the seeming impossibilities of your particular situation, you find yourself doubting. *Can my kids change the world? Other kids must have special opportunities or resources that my kids don't.* Maybe you're a single parent with very little time left over for investing in your kids. Maybe you look at your limited finances and wonder how you can give your kids special opportunities to make their God-dreams become a reality. Or maybe you have little involvement in your kids' lives due to circumstances beyond your control. But even in light of all these circumstances, something tells me that if I do my part to the best of my ability, I can leave the rest to the God who made my kids, and who says it's all very possible for them. No limitations and circumstances are about to stop the all-powerful God who parted a giant of a sea, and closed mouths of hungry lions, and even made the sun go backwards![9]

Pursue God-Dreams

"No one can kill your dreams," Papa once told me. "Joseph had a God-given dream that his entire family would bow down before him. His father scolded him, and his brothers were furious. They said, 'Here comes that dreamer! Come on, let's kill him and throw him into a deep pit. We can tell our father that a wild animal has eaten him. Then we'll see what becomes of all his dreams!' (Genesis 37:19–20). His brothers hated him and left him for dead, but they didn't keep him away from his dream, which resulted in the saving of a whole nation of people.

"Martin Luther King said, 'I have a dream!' He was killed pursuing that dream, but no one could kill his dream for civil rights in America.

"Abraham Lincoln had a dream to stop slavery in America. His enemies killed him, but they did not stop his dream.

"Jesus Christ had a dream to establish God's Kingdom among every people, tribe, nation, and language of this world (Revelation 7:9). His enemies killed him but they could never kill or destroy His dream."

Papa continued, "Your enemies, your 'friends,' and sometimes even family may be willing to leave you for dead in a ditch somewhere, but they cannot kill the dream you are willing to live and die for. I, too, have a God-given dream of establishing one million churches in the unreached parts of the world with the help of one million orphaned and abandoned street children. Like those before me, I too suffer because of this dream. There's a chance I will die for this dream, but nothing they do to me will stop this God-given dream. It is already happening."

Papa prays that many visionaries across the world will help him see this dream through. He says, "Let us not fall asleep on this God-dream until the last child who is willing has been shaped and sent as an arrow for God's Kingdom. The desire of every believer should be this: to see our relatives, neighbors, countrymen, and everyone we can think of enter into a saving relationship with Jesus. And to raise up children—our own and others—who will one day be a part of finishing the work of the Great

Commission. When we see that our dear ones are led to the Lord and that our children are impacting the world, what a great joy comes into our hearts."

What are the dreams you have for your children that you must not fall asleep on? Do you want the world to change your children, or are you willing to do what it takes for your children to change the world? You can't have it both ways. But as you have seen in our many visionaries and wise guides whose stories have been shared throughout this book, with some rearranging of priorities and adopting of a new mindset, we have all the tools and power we need within our reach to see these dreams through.

Andrew Murray inspires me with this idea: "I delight to give what is my most precious possession upon earth to be His. It is not only for God's sake, but for my child's sake that I give him to the Lord. The more I love my child, the more heartily I give him away to God. Nowhere can [my child] be safe or happy except with Him. And this is so wonderful—the child I give to God becomes doubly my own. The child I give to God, He holds for me and then gives him back again. Giving my child has become the link of a most blessed friendship and relationship between God and me."[10]

Yes, you love your children. And I love my children. But God loves them so much more. We *want* the very best for them, but only God can *give* the very best to them.

The Amazing Race Is On

Shucks and I have so wanted to do the *Amazing Race,* ever since viewing our first episode. We want to see the world, and we love challenges. We're both as competitive as "Mr. and Mrs. Smith," which, now that I think about it, might not be so great for our Christian witness in front of millions. But hey, after pioneering the great outback of Wyoming for so many years, we're pretty sure we could employ some of our finely-tuned survival skills in any country.

These days, we're not feeling quite so left out of The Race. We took a trip in 2007 to visit several of Papa's orphanages in northeast India and encountered many adventures that blew past many of the comparatively ho-hum A.R. stunts. We awakened before sunrise in remote villages to the sound of distant drums, jived with costume-clad kids to their tribal dance rituals, held our feet up while orphans washed them in their dinner bowls (a tribal custom to honor guests), took a morning bath in a remote Himalayan river, and interviewed humble pastors who bravely took beatings (and sometimes bullets) from anti-Christians.

We drew crowds in villages where they'd never seen white people. In one village, about two hundred men, women, children, goats, chickens, pigs, and dogs followed us as we explored, not unlike the Pied Piper. We strolled the streets during an annual, sacred "Festival of Lights," where the phenomenal light shows at night were a stark contrast to the primitive villages they bejeweled, and where intricately erected temples each housed an ominous goddess statue (a dark-skinned, Indian goddess slaying "a white female devil" to be exact—gulp).

We experienced the protection of angels when threatened by bandits and cobras the night our car broke down in the middle a deserted rice paddy, over a hundred miles from our destination. We witnessed the power of the Holy Spirit when we were unexpectedly called on to speak the Gospel message in front of a pagan village, where many received Christ, and again when we met with national dignitaries to plead on behalf of oppressed Christian ministries. We encouraged pastors in rebuilt tsunami villages on the Indian Ocean; experienced a warm welcome by prostitutes, sharing their food and holding their children when we visited their brothels in a major city; played cricket with state champion orphans; and my nearest death experience so far—drove in Calcutta traffic at rush hour!

Do we feel deprived by not qualifying for *The Amazing Race? Are you kidding?* (Please note: if you are an A.R. producer reading this, we're still willing to reconsider.)

What about you? Do you have an itch to forge out on a similar adventure, but you've just never gotten around to it? If you so choose, this kind of experience can easily be shared with your family, too. It can all be part of raising arrows, these kinds of life-changing trips, getting your family involved physically in *the mission*. But even if you're not inclined to travel the world on such daring adventures, you can still take part in a different sort of *Amazing Race* by becoming an arrow parent at home and beyond.

And here's a cool thought. On the Hollywood version of *The Amazing Race*, you race for a mere one million dollars. How lame is that compared to *God's Amazing Race*, where we're now actually racing for 1,000,000+ ARROWS—at least one million children, emerging from every continent—who grow up redeemed in God's love, ready and willing to bring that same love and hope back to their communities, cultures, and countries.

Remember we're racing with other families like the Harrises, the Tebows, the Andersons, and the Gaultieres. We're also racing with Papa, and with so many other dedicated arrow ministries. We're also racing with arrows like Willio in Haiti, Nick in Australia, Patrick in Europe, Jennie in India, Abigail and Danny in Israel, Ralph and Stella in Japan, Clayton in North Carolina, Paula in the Philippines, and so many others, each running together in a team effort in this truly *Amazing Race*!

Our families can become part of this God-given dream—part of Papa's vision. We can raise our kids to be arrows, and together, we can send arrows beyond who will finish the job that God gave us—offering every nation, tribe, people, and language a chance to hear and accept the Good News. As lives are touched worldwide, many people will find life-giving hope in God.

And best of all, we will watch our children grow up with mind-blowing purpose and passion, just like we always dreamed for them. If you are willing to accept the challenge of becoming an arrow parent, God will gladly take the opportunity of proving to you that it is the highest joy and most gratifying privilege that you could have chosen to pursue in this lifetime.

Will you become a part of Papa's dream to see *one million arrows* gathered, sharpened, and launched for God? Will you place arrows—both your own and those who have no earthly parents—in God's quiver to be used as a spiritual weapon against the kingdom of darkness? At the end of the race, will you hear, "Well done, my good and faithful servant, you have been faithful in handling this small amount, so now I will give you many more responsibilities. Come! Let's celebrate together!" (Matthew 25:21)?

Go Change the World

The Mighty Man pulled back the string of His bow, where the arrow He had shaped with loving hands drew in close to His heart, aimed at His target, and let go. Then He took another, and He did the same. Then another. He scattered His arrows—at least one million of them—all across the nations.

When they'd all hit their targets, His message was broadcast to the farthest reaches of the earth. He took a deep breath, smiled an unusually satisfied smile, stretched out His hands with pleasure, and proclaimed words that echoed across history, "It is finished."

Epilogue:
A Note from Papa

To my beloved reader,

Who is this Mighty Man, this Warrior, who wants His quiver full of arrows?" I looked up and saw a white horse. Its rider carried a bow, and a crown was placed on His head. He rode out to win many battles and gain the victory" (Revelation 6:2).

Only one Mighty Man in history fits this description—Jesus Christ. How wonderful it is to give our very own children into the hands of this Mighty Warrior and King of all kings to become arrows. He will use every single one placed into His hands for conquering the world with His love.

The Bible says happy and blessed is the man whose quiver is full of arrows to give to the Mighty Man. My parents, poor as they were, gave me into God's hands as His arrow to India, and they were blessed. I gave my own three children and 16,000 orphaned or abandoned children to the Lord, fully sharpened. I am also a blessed man.

Will you receive the blessing by giving your children into the hands of the Mighty King so they may truly help change the world with their gifts? Will you help support other children of the world that they may be launched as arrows to reach all who have not heard with the message of God's love?

Friend, arrows are not born or found on the road–they are made. It is a long, tedious, hard job. They must be put through fire, pounded, cut, shaped, and polished in order to be made worthy for the Master. Perhaps the size of the task is daunting, and it makes you afraid to try for fear of failure. Maybe you are afraid of offering yourself or your children to serve the Lord. If the fear is not gone from your heart, listen carefully to His words: "Don't be afraid, for I am with you. Do not be dismayed, for I am your God. I will strengthen you. I will help you. I will uphold you with my victorious right hand" (Isaiah 41:10).

As long as Christ reigns in your heart, you will never be a failure. He never made a single failure of those He called and who walked with and abided in Him. You will be able to challenge every person and every power under heaven that stands in your way of fulfilling His Word by making and sending arrows.

Go forward without fear. Go with the Lord and for the Lord. He promised that He will go with you, and you with God are the majority. No one can stand against you. Be strong and courageous when you go. Read and meditate upon the Word of God and obey it. Do not turn from it to the right or to the left.

Let us rise up and walk. This year is given to us not to sleep but to work for the Lord. Let us possess the world with the promised inheritance–the Good News of Jesus Christ reaching the world through His arrows.

All my love,

Papa

About the Author

Julie Ferwerda and her husband, Steve, challenge families nationwide to become part of a movement by using their God-given gifts and talents to make a significant spiritual impact in their schools, workplaces, and communities. They are both trained faculty members of CLASSEMINARS, INC., a professional communications development organization.

Recognized for making the Bible relevant to everyday life, Julie's writing is featured in many Christian magazines and websites. She hosts two regular blogs for Crosswalk.com and CBN.com, and she is the author of *The Perfect Fit: Piecing Together True Love.*

Julie is the mother of two teenage arrows, Danielle and Jessica, who are both making a significant spiritual impact in their school, peer groups, and community.

Near the completion of this book in December, 2008, Papa suffered a massive stroke when he came to the U.S. to raise money for his orphans, and is no longer able to speak or walk. He's in good spirits, though, and he still spends a lot of his day praying for the fulfillment of his *One Million Arrows Vision.*

Now, more than ever, Papa needs our voices to help to carry on his legacy. Visit our website to learn more about Papa and getting involved in his vision of orphan care, as well as resources for family growth and parenting world changers, arrow testimonies, and much more.

ONEMILLIONARROWS.COM

Julie with Papa in India, September 2008

A BIG THANK YOU

To all the individuals and families who inspired me on this journey, and who volunteered time, ideas, testimonies, and arrow-shaping techniques to be a part of this project, especially: Rod Morris; Gregg, Sono, Alex, and Brett Harris; Josh McDowell; Jack, Kim, Chloe, and Petra Anderson; Steve and Kristi Gaultiere; Joe, Jane, and Clayton King; Loyd and Renee Teakell; Paula Rollo; Ivan van Vuuren; Justin Dobrenz; Bart Pierce; Shannon Patrick; Craig Gross; J.R. Mahon; Kohl Crecelius; Jeremy West; Bob, Pam, and Tim Tebow; and Nick Vujicic.

Also many thanks to our overseas arrows who contributed their stories: Ralph and Stella Cox; Patrick McDonald; "Danny and Abigail"; Napoleon; "David and Anita"; Dan and Viji; Jenny; Lily; and Willio.

A huge thanks to Michele Huey and Helen Hunter for their amazing editorial services. Also to those who read and helped in the formation of the book: Sandy Ellingson, Robby Brumberg, Shelley Thomas, Clayton King, the Nickerson 10, Erin Garcia, Linda Goldfarb, Shannon Wall, Jami Kirkbride, Robin Stanley, Cheryl Pruitt, and Gerry Wakeland.

RESOURCES

Books for Family Spiritual Growth

One Year Bible, (NASB is more accurate, NLT is easier to understand).

The One Year Book of Josh McDowell's Family Devotions, (Tyndale Kids, 1997).

One Year Book of Family Devotions, Vol. 1, (Tyndale, 2000).

Gather Round the Dinner Fable, Steven James, (David C. Cook Publishers, 2006).

Dinner Table Devotions and Discussion Starters, Nancy Guthrie, (Tyndale, 2008).

The Christian Heroes Series, Janet and Geoff Benge, (YWAM Publishing, 1999).

The Treasure Principle: Unlocking the Secret of Joyful Giving, (Randy Alcorn, 2005).

The New Evidence Demands a Verdict: Answer the Questions Challenging Christians Today, (Josh McDowell, 1999).

Risking Faith: a 40-Day Journey into the Mystery of God (Dr. Steve Stephens, 2008).

Do Hard Things: a Teenage Rebellion Against Low Expectations (Alex and Brett Harris, 2008).

Join the Movement: God is Calling You to Change the World (Alvin L. Reid, 2007).

The Burning Heart Contract: a 21-day Challenge to Ignite Your Passion and Fulfill Your Purpose (Becky Tirabassi, 2005).

The Journals of Rachel Scott: a Journey of Faith at Columbine High (Beth Nimmo & Debra K. Klingsporn, 2001).

The Wild Goose Chase (Mark Batterson, 2008).

In A Pit With A Lion On A Snowy Day (Mark Batterson, 2006).

Don't Check Your Brains at the Door (Josh McDowell & Bob Hostetler, 1992).

Restoration: Returning the Torah of God to the Disciples of Jesus (D. Thomas Lancaster, 2005).

Websites for Family Growth Resources and Missions

Julie's Bible Commentary Guide for Families (www.onemillionarrows.com/OYB).

Julie's modern alternative to the Westminster Catechism (www.onemillionarrows.com/foundations).

Planet Wisdom (www.planetwisdom.com).

Caleb Resources, !Red Card: an 8-week family curriculum to help families understand God's heart for children at risk and how to make a difference in their lives (www.redcardkids.org).

Youth Bytes with Chad Daniel (www.youthbytes.org).

Nehemiah Institute for biblical worldview training (www.nehemiahinstitute.com).

The Vision Forum (www.visionforum.com).

The Rebelution, Alex and Brett Harris (www.therebelution.com).

Battle Cry, Ron Luce (www.battlecry.com).

Teen Mania Global Expeditions
(www.globalexpeditions.com).

Youth With A Mission (www.YWAM.org).

Crossroads Worldwide, Clayton King (www.claytonking.com and www.crossroadsworldwide.org).

El Shaddai Ministries: Messianic Jewish teachings for greater understanding of the Bible and prophecy
(www.elshaddaiministries.us).

Parenting Resources

One Million Arrows (www.onemillionarrows.com).

FamilyLife (www.familylife.com).

WisdomWorks Ministries (www.realworldparents.com).

Josh McDowell Ministries (www.josh.org).

Revolutionary Parenting: What the Research Shows Really Works (George Barna, 2007).

Family Driven Faith: Doing What it Takes to Raise Sons and Daughters who Walk with God (Voddie Baucham, 2007).

The Last Christian Generation (Josh McDowell and David H. Bellis, 2006).

Battle Cry for a Generation: The Fight to Save America's Youth (Ron Luce, 2005).

Raising Your Children for Christ (Andrew Murray, 1997).

Growing a Spiritually Strong Family (Dennis and Barbara Rainey, 2002).

Parenting Today's Adolescent: Helping your Child Avoid the Traps of the Preteen and Teen Years (Dennis and Barbara Rainey, Bruce Nygren, 2002).

Parenting with Love and Logic (a great discipline book, Foster W. Cline and Jim Fay, 2006).

Other Arrow or Featured Ministry Websites

Samaritan's Purse, Franklin Graham (www.samaritanspurse.org).

Voice of the Martyrs (www.persecution.com).

Xtreme Life Television, Ivan Van Vuuren (www.xtremelife.tv).

Krochet Kids International, Kohl Crecelius (www.krochetkids.org).

Life Without Limbs, Nick Vujicic (www.lifewithoutlimbs.org).

XXX Church (#1 Christian Porn Site, www.XXXChurch.com).

EQUIP (equipping leaders to reach our world) (www.iequip.org).

Vision Beyond Borders (www.vbbonline.org).

Rachel Joy Scott (www.racheljoyscott.com and www.rachelschallenge.com).

Bill and Kristi Gaultiere, Psychotherapy and Spiritual Mentoring (www.christiansoulcare.com).

Bob Tebow Evangelistic Association (www.btea.org).

Gregg and Sono Harris (www.nobleinstitute.org/ministries.php).

Restorers of Zion Ot-U'Mofet ("Danny and Abigail") (www.restorersofzion.org/restore_mofet.html).

Vision Beyond Borders (www.vbbonline.org).

Specialized Orphan Arrow Ministries (alphabetically, not all-inclusive)

Adoption Discovery, (www.adoptiondiscovery.com).

Tag line: Equipping families for new possibilities.

Unique ministry: Adoption Discovery is a 7-week small group curriculum that walks potential adoptive parents through the adoption process, helping them to better understand the process. Small groups and churches can get leader training to educate those in the body who are interested in adoption.

All Kids Can Learn International (www.akcli.org).

Unique ministry: Among other forms of orphan care, AKCLI is creating "villages of hope," self-sustaining models throughout Africa with commercial agricultural training centers, where orphans will become self-sustaining. *Mission trips available.*

Bethany Christian Services (www.bethany.org).

Unique ministry: A full service adoption ministry for both domestic and international adoption, orphan care, adoption support, infertility ministry, foster care, and estate planning.

Ministry locations: US, Eastern Europe, South Korea, China, Central America, Africa

Buckner International (www.buckner.org).

Unique ministry: For over 128 years, Buckner has been a leader in the movement toward justice for orphans and widows. Working in an advisory role with many international governments, BI educates leaders on children's issues and creates new legislature, ensuring lasting changes for at-risk children. *Mission trips available.*

Ministry locations: More than 50 countries worldwide

Caroline's Promise (www.carolinespromise4u.org).

Tag line: Reclaiming Hope for Orphans.

Unique ministry: Provides adoptive family assistance, orphan care, and adoption education for families. *Mission trips available.*

Christian Alliance for Orphans, (www.cryoftheorphan.com, www.christianalliancefororphans.org).

Tag line: Joining voices to care for orphans.

Unique ministry: With over 75 members, the CAO desires to see "every orphan experience God's unfailing love and knowing Jesus as Savior" through a united front among Christians, churches, and organizations.

Ministry locations: Network base United States, with partners worldwide

Crown Financial Ministries (www.crown.org).

Tag line: Teaching God's people how to make, manage, and fulfill in every nation.

Unique Ministry: Crown equips people worldwide to learn, apply, and teach God's financial principles so they may know Christ more intimately, be free to serve Him, and help fund the Great Commission.

Every Orphan's Hope, (www.everyorphan.org).

Tag line: Sharing the love of Jesus Christ with orphaned children in Africa.

Unique ministry: To love, protect, and care for orphans affected by the HIV/AIDS pandemic through sponsorship, homes, evangelism, and discipleship. *Mission trips available.*

Ministry locations: Zambia, Africa

Food for Orphans (www.foodfororphans.org).

Tag line: Saving lives . . . one meal at a time.

Unique ministry: FFO exists to make sure that every orphan receives at least one nutritious meal per day. They support orphan care programs that historically care for needs of orphans yet struggle to provide the necessary food.

Ministry locations: Asia, Africa, Central America, South America, Caribbean

Forgotten Children International (www.forgottenchildren.org).

Tag line: Assisting the forgotten children around the globe.

Unique ministry: FCI provides housing construction grants for orphan homes and collects and ships used clothing in shipping containers around the globe.

Ministry locations: Africa, India, Ukraine

God's Kids, (www.godskids.com).

Tag line: Giving orphans hope and a future.

Unique ministry: An orphan ministry "watchdog," GK raises the standard of care and accountability for orphanages around the world in quality nutrition, clean residences, and adequate medical care so orphans can become significant contributors to their society.

Ministry locations: Mexico, Burma, Philippines, Cambodia, India, Liberia

Hope for Orphans (www.hopefororphans.org).

Tag line: Serving every church to reach every orphan.

Unique ministry: This FamilyLife ministry serves churches in order to mobilize believers, equip church leaders to develop orphan ministries, and to connect churches to key orphan ministries in order to care for orphans.

Hopegivers International (www.hopegivers.org).

Tag line: Help for today, hope for eternity.

Unique ministry: Fulfilling Dr. M.A. Thomas's (Papa's) "One Million Orphan-Arrow Vision" by gathering at least one million orphaned and abandoned children, sharpening them, and then launching them back into their societies to fulfill the Great Commission. *Mission trips available.*

Ministry locations: India, Malawi (Africa), Haiti

Kids Alive International (www.kidsalive.org).

Tag line: Christian care for children at risk.

Unique ministry: Since 1916, KAI rescues suffering children in crisis, nurturing them with quality holistic care, and introducing them to Jesus Christ so they can offer hope to others. *Mission trips available.*

Ministry locations: Africa, Asia, Latin America, Eastern Europe, Middle East

Loving Shepherd Ministries (www.loving-shepherd.org).

Unique ministry: A premier adoption resource center, LSM provides free information to anyone seeking Christ-centered adoption. In addition, they design, build, and operate homes for orphans worldwide and provide corrective surgeries for needy orphans in developing countries.

Orphan Outreach (www.orphanoutreach.org).

Tag line: Provides a "voyage of hope" for orphans around the world.

Unique ministry: In addition to a variety of orphan care, OO offers "Mission Backpack," where children are given a backpack full of essentials including a Bible, to remind each child that they never walk alone. *Mission trips available.*

Ministry Locations: Guatemala, India, Honduras, Russia

Red Letters Campaign (www.redletterscampaign.com).

Tag line: Living faith to end poverty.

Unique ministry: The Red Letters Campaign is a self-funded, volunteer led community of like-minded families mobilizing the church to bring care and assistance to the world's most vulnerable through engaging projects and interactive community experiences. They aim to connect their members with others who share their passions, provide resources to equip the community, and connect that greater community with qualified front-line partners to improve the lives of the suffering around the world.

Red Letters Campaign for Kids
(www.redletterscampaign.com/blogs/kids/pages/rlc_5F00_kids.aspx).

Tag line: Raising kids to change the world.

Unique ministry: RLC Kids believes that there is no age or height requirement on living compassionately! Their community provides both a platform for families to exchange ideas on teaching their children about living compassion and a place to find fun, safe projects that put children in the driver's seat to change the lives of children around the world.

Shaohannah's Hope (www.shaohannahshope.org).

Tag line: Mobilizing the body of Christ to care for orphans.

Unique ministry: Engaging the church to care for orphans and helping Christian families reduce the financial barrier to adoption. *Mission trips available.*

Vision Trust International (www.visiontrust.org).

Tag line: Hope for the world's neediest children.

Unique ministry: Enabling Christian nationals to meet the physical, educational, emotional, and spiritual needs of orphaned and neglected children in order to produce mature Christians in their own culture. *Mission trips available.*

Ministry locations: Latin America, Caribbean, Africa, Asia

Viva Network, Patrick McDonald (www.viva.org).

Tag line: Working together to bring more children better care.

Unique ministry: Working to map the world of Christian care for children by 2014 and to cause a revolution by: empowering connections, preventing duplication, and identifying need.

Ministry locations: Regional centers in England, Asia, Africa, and Latin America

Warm Blankets Orphan Care Intl. (www.warmblankets.org, www.traffickinginpersons.com).

Tag line: Don't let traffickers get the orphans first!

Unique ministry: WB restores lives in partnership with churches, corporations, organizations, and individuals who have a passion to help needy, parentless children. In addition, they rescue and protect vulnerable children who would otherwise become trafficking victims.

Ministry locations: Asia, Africa

World Orphans (www.worldorphans.org).

Tag line: ec3—Each church. Each child. Each community.

Unique ministry: WO is committed to rescuing millions of orphaned and abandoned children, strengthening thousands of indigenous churches, and impacting hundreds of communities with the Gospel of Jesus Christ in the least reached areas of the world. *Mission trips available.*

Ministry locations: Asia, Africa, Latin America, Eastern Europe, India, Middle East

ENDNOTES

Chapter 1: Determine Your Course

[1] William Jennings Bryan, "Famous Quotes and Authors": *www.famous-quotesandauthors.com/authors/william_jennings_bryan_quotes.html*.

[2] Cary Sheih, "The Survival Story of Cary Sheih" *NewYork-Stories.com: www.newyork-stories.com/cpo/911/detail.php?nr=145&kategorie =911* (March 2008).

[3] Friso Paping, Tolga Paksoy, Pieter Heslenfeld, "Lifesaver Hero: Firemen of 9/11" *MyHero.com: www.myhero.com/myhero/hero.asp?hero=Firemen_schr_NL_07_ul* (March 2008).

[4] Cary Sheih, "The Survival Story of Cary Sheih," *NewYork-Stories.com: www.newyork-stories.com/cpo/911 /detail.php?nr=145&kategorie =911* (March 2008).

[5] Dawn Eden, "Think big! High School Bloggers Tell Peers," *New York Daily News* (August 28, 2005).

Chapter 2: Join the Vision

[1] Dr. M.A. Thomas, taken from an interview in India (September 2008).

2 Voddie Baucham Jr., *Family Driven Faith* (Illinois: Crossway Books, 2007), 158.

3 Dennis Rainey, from a keynote address at the Cry of the Orphan Summit, Ft. Lauderdale, FL, May 1–3, 2008.

4 Andrew Murray, *Raising Your Children for Christ* (Pennsylvania: Whitaker House, 1984), 71–72.

Chapter 3: Own the Mission

1 Alvin Reid, *Join the Movement: God is calling you to change the world* (Kregel Publications, 2007), 36.

2 Ivan Van Vuuren, comment in e-mail interview (March 2005).

3 Frederick Buechner, *Wishful Thinking: A Seeker's ABC* (HarperOne; Rev Exp edition, 1993).

4 Mark Batterson, *Wild Goose Chase* (Multnomah Books, 2008), 16.

5 Nick Vujicic, *www.lifewithoutlimbs.org/about-nick-vujicic.php* (April 20, 2008).

6 Ibid (Vujicic).

7 Mark Batterson, *Wild Goose Chase* (Multnomah Books, 2008), 23–24.

8 Sarah Haas, *No Yarn: Young Men Do Good with Stitch in Time* MSNBC, Sept. 20, 2007, *www.msnbc.msn.com/id/20780105* (Dec. 23, 2008).

9 Jason Rovou, *'Porn & Pancakes' fights X-rated Addictions*, CNN.com, April 6, 2007, *www.cnn.com/2007/US/04/04/porn.addiction/index. html* (June 2008).

10 Ibid (Rovou).

11 Martin Bashir, "*The Porn Pastors: XXXChurch.com*" ABC News February 2, 2007, *abcnews.go.com/print?id=2841065* (June 2008).

12 Mark Batterson, *Wild Goose Chase*, (Multnomah Books, 2008), 145.

Chapter 4: Gather Broken Branches

1 Andrew Murray, *Raising Your Children for Christ* (Pennsylvania: Whitaker House, 1984), 65.

2 Nancy Grace, "Transcripts," CNN.com, December 6, 2006, *transcripts. cnn.com/TRANSCRIPTS/0612/06/ng.01.html*, (July 19, 2008).

3 T.C. Pinkney, *Report to the Southern Baptist Convention Executive Committee*, Nashville, TN, Sept. 18, 2001. Report of the Southern Baptist Council of Family Life (2002).

4 George Barna, *A Biblical Worldview Has a Radical Effect on a Person's Life* (The Barna Group, 2003), *wwwbarna.org/FlexPage.aspx?Page=Barna Update&BarnaUpdateID=154*.

5 Ron Luce, *Battle Cry for a Generation: The Fight to Save America's Youth* (Colorado Springs: Cook Communications, 2005), 29.

6 Alvin Reid, *Raising the Bar: Ministry to Youth in the New Millennium* (Grand Rapids, MI: Kregel, 2004).

7 Ibid (Reid).

8 George Barna, *Revolutionary Parenting* (Tyndale House Publishers, Inc., 2007), xvii.

9 George Barna, *Revolutionary Parenting* (Tyndale House Publishers, Inc., 2007), 11.

10 Voddie Baucham Jr., *Family Driven Faith* (Crossway Books, 2007), 177, 182.

11 Josh McDowell, *The Last Christian Generation* (Holiday, FL: Green Key Books, 2006), 11.

12 The Barna Group, *Parents Accept Responsibility for Their Child's Spiritual Development But Struggle With Effectiveness, wwww.barna.org/FlexPage.a spx?Page=BarnaUpdate&BarnaUpdateID=138* (July 28, 2008).

13 George Barna, *Revolutionary Parenting* (Tyndale House Publishers, Inc., 2007), 38.

14 Bart Pierce, quotes taken from phone interview (July 28, 2008).

Chapter 5: Shape Arrows at Home

1 Andrew Murray, *Raising Your Children for Christ* (Pennsylvania: Whitaker House, 1984), 131.

2 Pete Thamel, "The Quad," *The New York Times* (Sept. 12, 2007), *http://thequad.blogs.nytimes.com/2007/09/12/tim-tebow-visits-the-quad-a/index.html?ref=sports* (February 12, 2008).

3 Barbara Denman, "Tebow's Commitment to Honoring God Supersedes his Athletic Success," *Florida Baptist Convention*: *www.flbaptist.org/news/fbc_news_Tebow_honors_God.htm* (February 12, 2008).

4 Ibid (Denman).

5 Ibid (Denman).

6 Joe Henderson, "A Humble Side," Tampa Bay Online, December 7, 2007, *www2.tbo.com/content/2007/dec/07/na-a-humble-side/?sports-colleges-gators* (February 12, 2008).

7 Child training principles by Bog and Pam Tebow taken and compiled from cited articles.

8 Joe Henderson, "A Humble Side," *Tampa Tribune* (December 7, 2007), *www2.tbo.com/content/2007/dec/07/na-a-humble-side/?sports-colleges-gators* (February 12, 2008).

9 Ibid (Henderson).

10 Josh McDowell, notes from a seminar given to parents at Autumn Ridge Church, Rochester, MN (September 2007).

11 Ibid.

12 Ibid.

13 George Barna, *Revolutionary Parenting* (Tyndale House Publishers, Inc., 2007), 71–72.

14 Gregg and Sono Harris, all quotes and training ideas taken from phone interview (January 16, 2008).

15 Kristi Gaultiere, all quotes and training ideas taken from phone interview (March 4, 2008).

16 Jack and Kim Anderson, all quotes and training ideas taken from phone interview (February 25, 2008).

Chapter 6: Shape Arrows Beyond

[1] John Piper, "Let the Nations be Glad!" in *Perspectives on the World Christian Movement*, ed. Stephen C. Hawthorne and Ralph D. Winter, 3d ed. (Pasadena, CA: William Carey, 1999), 54.

[2] Edward Lorenz, "Butterfly Effect," *en.wikipedia.org/wiki/Butterfly_effect* (April 19, 2009).

[3] Teen Mania Global Expeditions, "A Note to Parents," *www.globalexpeditions.com/parents.php* (March 2009).

[4] YWAM, "About YWAM and YWAM Explained," *www.ywam.org/contents/abo_wha_ywamexplained.htm* (March 2009).

[5] Jennie (one of Papa's adopted daughters), all quotes taken from an interview in Kota, India (November 2008).

[6] Lily, all quotes taken from an interview in a tribal village in Jharkhand, India (November 2008).

[7] Shannon Patrick, all quotes taken by interview in person (July, 2008).

Chapter 7: Mobilize Bows

[1] Loren Eiseley, from the essay, "The Star Thrower," *The Unexpected Universe* (Harcourt, Brace and World, 1969).

[2] Randy Alcorn, *The Treasure Principle: Unlocking the Secret of Joyful Giving* (Multnomah Publishers, Inc.), 44.

[3] John L. Ronovalle and Sylvia Ronsvalle, *The State of Church Giving through 2000* (Champaign, Ill.: Empty Tomb, 2002), 13.

[4] John L. Ronsvalle and Sylvia Ronsvalle, *The State of Church Giving through 2000* (Champaign, Ill.: Empty Tomb, 2002), 54.

Chapter 8: Count the Cost

[1] Andrew Murray, *Raising Your Children for Christ* (Whitaker House, 1984), 110.

[2] Johann Christof-Arnold, *Seeking Peace* (Plume, 2000).

[3] Dr. M.A. Thomas, "Martyr's Pledge," recited by his graduating Bible college students.

[4] Steven James, *Sailing Between the Stars: musings on the mysteries of faith* (Revell, September 2006), 184–185.

[5] Beth Nimmo & Debra K. Klingsporn, *The Journals of Rachel Scott: A Journey of Faith at Columbine High* (Thomas Nelson, 2001).

[6] Rachel's Challenge, *www.rachelschallenge.com* (April 7, 2009).

[7] "Danny and Abigail" are pseudo names to protect their ministry. All quotes were taken by e-mail interview (December, 2008).

Chapter 9: Keep Your Eyes on the Prize

[1] Randy Alcorn, *The Treasure Principle: Unlocking the Secret of Joyful Giving* (Sisters: Multnomah Publishers, 2001), 19.

[2] Dan and Viji Gupta, all information taken from personal interview and time spent in the couple's home in South India (November 2008).

[3] William Carey (missionary), Wikipedia, *en.wikipedia.org/wiki/ William_Carey.*

[4] Randy Alcorn, *The Treasure Principle: Unlocking the Secret of Joyful Giving* (Multnomah Publishers, Inc.), 46, 13.

Chapter 10: Land a Bull's-Eye, Change the World

[1] Alvin Reid, *Join the Movement: God is Calling You to Change the World* (Grand Rapids: Kregel Publications, 2007), 26, 52.

[2] Malcolm McDow and Alvin L. Reid, *Firefall: How God Has Shaped History Through Revivals* (Nashville: Broadman and Holman, 1997); and J. Edwin Orr, *Campus Aflame: A History of Evangelical Awakenings in Collegiate Communities,* ed. Richard Owen Robers, new and rev. ed. (Wheaton, IL: International Awakening Press, 1994).

[3] Jeremy West, "Why I Joined a Gay Club," interview by Chris Lutes and Karen Raad, *Campus Life* (September/October 2000, Vol. 59, No. 2): 63.

[4] Chloe Anderson, all quotes taken by phone interview (February 25, 2008).

[5] Clayton King, all quotes taken by phone interview (March 5, 2008).

[6] Paula Cornette Rollo, all quotes taken by e-mail interview (March 10, 2008).

[7] C.S. Lewis, "Priceless Treasures: Why I Choose to Home School," by Gregg Harris, *greggharrisblog.blogspot.com* November 16, 2005, accessed April 7, 2009.

[8] George Barna, *Revolutionary Parenting*, (Tyndale House Publishers, Inc., 2007), 146.

[9] See Exodus 14:21–31; Daniel 6:11–24; Isaiah 38:1–8.

[10] Andrew Murray, *Raising Your Children for Christ* (Whitaker House, 1984), 107–108.

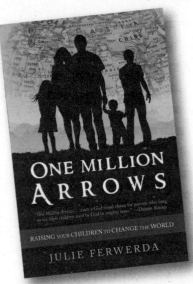

To order additional copies of *One Million Arrows*, please visit:

OneMillionArrows.com

All proceeds from the sale of *One Million Arrows* are designated for international orphan ministry work.

If you are a church or ministry, you can order as many copies as you'd like at cost (10 copy minimum).

Visit

OneMillionArrows.com

Where you'll find:

- inspirational blogs
- how-to Arrow parenting articles and ideas
- family growth tools
- user contributed stories of Arrows
- a valuable resources and link directory
- parenting community forum
- conference and event information
- orphan and adoption ministry spotlight
- information about Papa and his Arrows
- and much more